Everything is Happening For a Reason

The Definitive World View
for the
Third Millennium and Beyond

The Aqua Oracle: Book I

Lee Janisson

CROWN OAK PRESS

Acknowledgements

This book is dedicated to the Lord Jesus Christ, the Savior of the World, who is always our faithful and true High Priest.

J. Preston Eby has been a large influence in opening my eyes and setting me on the right track of understanding the Biblical truth of Universal Restoration. In 1988, I was given his small booklet titled: *Just What Do You Mean...Eternity?* - which was the pivotal point that set me on a fresh scriptural quest. Over the course of four years, I was transformed from being a staunch advocate of Eternal Damnation, to an absolute believer in Universal Restoration. That same booklet can now be found on the Internet at: www.godfire.net/eby/eternity_eby.html.

Since 1976, the instrumental mastery and lyrical finesse of Rush, the legendary arena-rockers - from Toronto Canada, have been the soundtrack for my life. Their anthems have supplied endless energy and inspiration during much of the fifteen years of research and writing of this book. Neil Peart, the drummer and lyricist for Rush, is without hesitation, my favorite poet. Various songs from some of their seventeen studio albums, have been integrated into this book as prologues to each chapter.

When I first listened to their album 2112 at the age of thirteen, Rush immediately became my favorite band, and will remain so. The following is a portion from that album, and the theme of this book. To learn more about Rush, log on to www.rush.com

V. Oracle: The Dream

I wandered home through the silent streets
And fell into a fitful sleep
Escape to realms beyond the night
Dream can't you show me the light

I stand atop a spiral stair
An oracle confronts me there
He leads me on light years away
Through astral nights, galactic days
I see the works of gifted hands
That grace this strange and wondrous land
I see the hand of man arise
With hungry mind and open eyes

They left the planet long ago
The elder race still learn and grow
Their power grows with purpose strong
To claim the home where they belong
Home to tear the Temples down…
Home to change!

And it shall come to pass in the last days, that the mountain
of the Lord's house
shall be established in the top of the mountains, and shall
be exalted above the hills; and all the nations shall flow
unto it.

And many people shall go and say, Come ye, and let us go
up to the mountain of the Lord, to the house of the God of
Jacob; and he will teach us of his ways,
And we will walk in his paths: for out of Zion shall go forth
the law,
and the word of the Lord from Jerusalem.

And he shall judge among the nations, and shall rebuke
many people:
and they shall beat their swords into plowshares, and their
spears into pruninghooks: nation shall not lift up sword
against nation, neither shall they learn war any more.

Isaiah 2:2-4

Table of Contents

Introduction

The Music of the Spheres is a phrase which first romanced my imagination through a song by Rush called - The Analog Kid. Years later, I discovered this expression originated in 600 B.C. with the mathematician and philosopher, Pythagoras, who believed our universe was flowing in divine harmony.

This is consistent with the ancient oracle found in Ephesians 1:11: *God works all things after the counsel of His own will.* If we believe that God is sovereign - then indeed: Everything is happening for a reason. The Creator of the Universe - the Uncaused Cause, the Infinite Center, is in control of Everything.

One of the existential questions that continues to echo around the planet is: If God is a loving God, why is there evil in the world? The answer is: Nothing can exist without it's opposite. Without evil, we would have no distinction to determine what is good. We only know that a towel is dry - when it's not wet. Without polarities in the universe, Yin and Yang, there is no frame of reference.

The world community is nearly out of the woods of the Dark Ages of the Crisis of Perception. The Ivory Towers of the death-inducing religions of mortal man are beginning to collapse, as their deception-laden dogmas are being dismantled. The luminescence of the new era of our spiritual reality is in acceleration —which some are calling the *Age of Aquarius*. I like the bumper-sticker that reads: My Karma Ran Over My Dogma. To remove any trace of suspicion - this is not the watered-down new age of "christ consciousness." Alternately, this is the New Age of the Consciousness of Jesus Christ – The New Age of Jesus Christ.

The prophetic pages of the Old and New Testament foretell of the time when peace shall reign on earth. The universally unifying influence that shall assist in bringing this into actualization, is when the international village begins to believe with absolution that everything is happening for a reason - that what we sow, we are going to reap, that Cause and Effect is truly a universal law, and ultimately, that Jesus Christ —The Alpha and Omega, is Lord.

We are right now in the time spoken of in Acts 3:19-21: Repent ye therefore, and be converted, that your sins may be blotted out, when times of refreshing shall come from the presence of the Lord; and he shall send Jesus Christ, which before was preached unto you: Whom the heaven must receive until the times of restitution of all things, which God hath spoken by the mouth of all his holy prophets since the world began.

This passage is a counterpoint which looms in opposition against the Eternal Damnation doctrine espoused by many religious institutions today. This misguided ideology emerged from major mistranslations in the Bible, driven by the Roman Empire around the fourth century. In the aftermath, the nations of the Earth have been led into a dark and distorted vortex – far from understanding the true nature of the plan of God.

Some may attempt to assuage others that the assertions in this book are merely my own viewpoints, opinions, and interpretations. Since water takes the path of least resistance, my answer is: Yes, and their conclusions lead to the full volume of The Music of the Spheres within us = Experiencing the fullness of the presence of God = Entering the Holy of Holies of spiritual growth - that we all would be made whole, spirit, soul, and body.

The Bible is a spiritual book inspired by the Holy Spirit for our spiritual growth. Year after year, it's the number-one-best-seller. At the same time, it is my conviction that the Bible has also been one of the least understood books in the world. It is my hope and prayer that *The Aqua Oracle* will help shed some light on many of the questions you have in revealing the ultimate intention of God for your life.

Along the river
March 2004

And they saw the God of Israel: and there was under his feet as it were a paved work of a sapphire stone, and as it were the body of heaven in his clearness.

Exodus 24:10

The Lord thy God, in the midst of thee is mighty; He will save, He will rejoice over thee with joy, He will rest in his love, He will joy over thee with singing.
Zephaniah 3:17

The end of the Lord is tender mercy.
James 5: 11b

Mystic Rhythms
Album: Power Windows

So many things I think about
When I look far away
Things I know - things I wonder
Things I'd like to say
The more we think we know about
The greater the unknown
We suspend our disbelief
And we are not alone -

Mystic rhythms - capture my thoughts
And carry them away
Mysteries of night
Escape the light of day
Mystic rhythms - Under northern lights
Or the African sun
Primitive things stir
The hearts of everyone

We sometimes catch a window
A glimpse of what's beyond
Was it just imagination
Stringing us along?
More things than are dreamed about
Unseen and unexplained
We suspend our disbelief
And we are entertained -

Mystic rhythms - capture my thoughts
And carry them away
Nature seems to spin
A supernatural way
Mystic rhythms - Under city lights
Or a canopy of stars
We feel the powers
And we wonder what they are

We feel the push and pull
Of restless rhythms from afar

CHAPTER ONE

Everything is Happening
For A Reason

There is no way to peace, peace is the way.
- A.J. Mustre

Envision the game show - *Let's Make A Deal*. Behind one of the three doors awaits the magic of Life - the secret of the universe:

Door #1: Nothing is happening for a reason.
Door #2: Something's are happening for a reason.
Door #3: Everything is happening for a reason.

On a stormy Saturday afternoon in the summer of 1996, when I would have preferred to be on the golf course or water-skiing, I found myself lying on the sofa, clicking the remote for something to watch on television. What I tuned into was the Summer Olympics. There was a middle-aged woman who had just finished a track-race which she did not win - being interviewed by a network journalist. While sitting down, trying to catch her breath as she was untying her running shoes, she casually said, "I guess everything happens for a reason." This was a woman who made running her career and way of life. Her ultimate goal was Olympic Gold - suddenly her dream was lost.

Now and then we hear the expression - "Everything happens for a reason." This axiom is usually stated after something unfortunate has transpired. The recipient of some unfortunate episode, understandably attempts to make sense of it all - by believing there must be some greater cause behind the misfortune, which will be of benefit to them in the long run. For instance, in the movie *Bruce Almighty*, after Bruce is fired from his position as a news anchor, his wife responds by saying, "Everything happens for a reason." In the movie *Shadowlands*, C.S. Lewis is lecturing in a European university concerning the negative events we encounter in our lives. His analogy to make sense of it all, was encapsulated something like this: " If it were not for the blows of the chisel on the stone, the sculpture would never come into being."

If I ever had a moment of awakening, it was that rainy afternoon on the sofa. Several days later, after meditating on this thought, I pulled out a notebook and wrote:

> *Everything is happening for a reason, there*
> *are only two other options:*
> 1. *Nothing is happening for a reason.*
> 2. *Something's are happening for a*
>   *reason.*

The fact that we are considering the three alternatives, is the effect of the cause of reading the three possibilities - immediately eliminating: Nothing happens for a reason.

We are now left with: Something's happen for a reason, and, Everything happens for a reason. To believe something's happen for a reason, broaches the inevitable two-part question:

First: What is the reason why something's happen for a reason?
Second: What is the reason why something's do not happen for a reason?

Nihilism is the worldview that suggests there is no meaning to the universe. Those with nihilistic notions, may suggest that there is no reason or order in the universe; that there does not need to be a reason; that not everything is reasonable or rational; that luck, chance, serendipity, or, arbitrariness, is the reason why something's happen, which of course are reasons.

To believe something's happen for a reason does not presuppose that all events leading up to those comprehendible realities in our lives, were not flowing in symphonic harmony up to the point of our comprehension. We can use words such as arbitrary, relative, luck, chance, or, mystery, to define events in our lives. However, to limit our concentration there, leaves us standing still in the dust of existential inertia. The Urantia Book states: The expansion of our spiritual horizon is broadened equally with the modifications and adjustments of our thoughts.

Everything Is Absolute

To believe that everything is relative, is to not believe everything is absolute. Confined within the context at hand, the dictionary definition of the word – relative, means - not absolute. The opposite of Nothing is Everything. The opposite of Relative is Absolute. We have already established that - *Nothing happens for a reason,* does not exist. Should we then freely assume that - Something is now the opposite of

Everything? If so, is it illogical to conclude the following:

Everything is Absolute equates to - Everything Is
    Happening For A Reason.
Everything is Relative equates to – Something's
    Happen For A Reason.

Absolute Relativity means everything is relative. This ideology presupposes the absoluteness that - Something's are happening for a reason. Which in turn, assumes absolutely that there is a reason why - Something's do not happen for a reason. The conflicted nature of believing that Everything is Relative, and that - Something's happen for a reason, removes itself from the context of the rational thought of science and scripture.

To press the limit, and transmute into the assertion that - Something's are Relative - presumes again, that everything else is Absolute. This regression remains unscientific and unscriptural. The British author, Iain Sinclair said, "An involuntary return to the point of departure is without doubt, the most disturbing of all journeys."

Maybe Albert Einstein's *Theory of Relativity*, should have a name change - *The Theory of Absolutes*. After all, he was attempting to show how all things hold together - not some thing's. To announce that Everything is Relative, is a concession that gray zones exist in life, which is an admission of our inability to comprehend the mysterious modes of the Universe. At the same time, would we have it any other way? Who would want to live in a world of the monotonous sequences of predictable events?

This leaves us standing at the final door, a threshold slowly opening to the clean air of ETHFAR, the acronym for Every Thing Happens For A Reason.

The Scientific Signature of God

Personally, I believe in the *Evolution of Creation* - that the continuum of Creation is evolving by the hand of our Creator. One thought which needs to be interjected into the Evolution vs. Creation debate is this: Genesis 1:14-19 announces that God created the sun, moon, and stars on the fourth day. Since the sun and moon are the two luminaries that set the stage for how we gauge time, the first three days of creation could have been untold billions of years. This provides much latitude and breathing room for the scientific data that supports the idea that the Earth was not created in six literal days, but over billions of years according to the timetable cast on the fourth day.

The Sciences support the axiom of ETHFAR. Within the scientific context, there are several reasons to believe nothing happens without a reason. Life on earth at times is seemingly random and irrational. The following universal laws or theories of physics, provide a glimpse into the universe, as being systematic and rational:

Sir Isaac Newton's Third Law of Motion: <u>For every action there is an equal and opposite</u> <u>reaction</u>. "Celestial Mechanics is the branch of physics formulated primarily by Sir Isaac Newton, to enable us to describe and predict the forces influencing both the actions and gravitational attractions of planets, stars and all other objects and living things in space." – Monte Farber

Albert Einstein's Unified Field Theory: <u>The universe is</u> <u>an unfolding evolutionary system governed by a creative</u> <u>principle that connects all things</u>. Some scientists today are expanding on the Unified Field Theory and no longer call it a *theory*, but rather, are so certain of it's truth, they have dropped the word theory, and call it – The Grand Unified Field. Others believe that it will never be proven. If the Grand Unified Field is never proven scientifically, it's because the computer industry will never be able to create software which can encapsulate the never-ending nature of infinity. Albert Einstein said – God does not roll dice.

The First Law of Thermodynamics: <u>Energy cannot be created or destroyed, it can only change from one form to another</u>. This Law of Thermodynamics is in harmony with Newton's Third Law; in that it shows the universe to be in a constant state of movement from order into disorder and back to order again, which is the action-reaction or yin and yang nature of creation.

Theory of Synchronicity: Dr. Carl Jung, the late German psychologist believed -<u>Everything that occurs has a relationship of significance called - Meaningful</u> <u>Coincidence.</u> All of us on different occasions experience coincidences. Sometimes they are helpful; other times they are humorous and even strange. Everything that happens to us in the external world, is a mirror reflection of what is really going on in our subconscious – the visible and invisible worlds are choreographing each other.

In my research at libraries, book stores, and on the Internet, to find scientific support for ETHFAR, my favorite non-Biblical discovery was a book by F. David Peat, entitled: *Synchronicity – The Bridge Between Matter and Mind.* I highly recommend it.

<u>The Flux Theory</u>: According to James Clifford Cranwell's book, *The Flux Theory 101: Properties of Energy & Matter – Common Knowledge in the 21st Century*, we can understand Gravity, Mass, Particle shapes, The Double Slit Experiment, The Four Forces, The Fifth Force, Fringe Patterns, Dark Matter, Missing Matter in the Universe, Binding energy, Alpha Beta Gamma Radiation, Atomic Structures, Induced Fields, Interference, Photo Electric Effect, Polarization of Light, Wave / Particle Duality, Zeeman Effect, Zero-point Energy, Why Superstring theories work mathematically in ten dimensions (currently they are

saying, 26 dimensions), Previously unknown effects, Constants and Theories of others. Cranwell says, "the Grand Unified Field might be a geometric problem and the Flux Theory is the solution."

Where Science and The Spirit integrate

According to the Physic's community, Super-strings are what the universe is made up of. Molecules are made up of atoms; atoms are made up of strings. Physicists tell us that super-strings are hyper-microscopic filaments of vibrating energy. To understand how small these strings are, consider this: If a single string was the size of a tree, an atom would be the size of the Milky Way. It is my conviction that the energy that the strings are made up of is Chi (Qi), the Chinese term for Life Force. It is my extended conviction - that the Life Force, is the subtle energy of the presence of God, "in whom all things consist" (Colossians 1:17).

All creation is the interconnection of super-strings playing together as a symphony, orchestrated through the creative will of God; this is - The Music of the Spheres. Creation is the eternal expression of infinity. Infinity is God. God is infinity. God is the Infinite and Eternal Source and Center, the Beginning and the End and everything in between.

Scientific theories or laws may casually hold my interest for a minute or two (evidenced by the extremely brief elaborations above) before I begin to yawn, then turn my attention to staring at the ceiling tiles. I would rather make myself a tuna-fish sandwich and go down the road kicking rocks believing in the Unified Field of Infinity. I have found using the Internet search engine - *Google*, helpful in exploring the theories or laws above.

In an esoteric context, there are several reasons to believe in ETHFAR:

Mystically: Yin and Yang.

Most Universally: The Law of Cause and Effect, often referred to as the Law of Karma.

Biblically: What you sow, you shall reap.

In Slang: What goes around comes around, or, What goes up must come down.

On July 1, 2002, I was encouraged to see the well-known international guru - Deepak Chopra, featured on *Pinnacle,* a show on CNN which interviews successful entrepreneurs. Mr. Chopra made the remark: "Nothing is coincidence, nothing is random."
Indeed, Deepak, everything is a coincidence, or, nothing is a coincidence.

It's All Music

"Everything Is Happening For A Reason" resonates in the subconscious in all of us. When the conscious mind centers it's focus on this thought, the harmonizing of the subconscious and conscious mind will be set in motion. We begin moving beyond the duality of heart and mind, into singularity, where our heart and mind become one: a single sphere. This is known as entering The Music of the Spheres.
This singularity, also moves us beyond the duality of past and future. We begin living in The Now: The continual present moment manifestations of the infinite —The Infinite Now. A Zen axiom I appreciate is: *Remain in the Nowhere Else – Be Here.* Spiritual growth can be measured by an increase of the volume of the Music of the Spheres within us. We begin to sense time slowing down, life becomes

more peaceful. This peace, is the music of the Music of the Spheres, the presence of God who fills all in all.

Interestingly, Pythagoras, who coined the term - The Music of the Spheres, lived in the same century as the prophet Daniel who wrote: Seal the book, even to the time of the end: many shall run to and fro, and knowledge shall be increased (Daniel 12:4). For every action there is an equal and opposite reaction; in the same era when Daniel is told to seal these things, Pythagoras is unsealing the Music of the Spheres.

God Does Not Believe in Atheists

When discussing the existence or non-existence of God, there is a maneuver to prove Atheists do not exist: Envision a circle - inside the circle is all the knowledge known to man since the dawn of civilization. Ask an atheist: Do you believe you have all knowledge? Atheists must make the admission: "I know there is no God." If they are honest, they will concede that they do not have all knowledge. Then tell them: "Ok, I'm going to be liberal with you – let's say you have eighty percent of all knowledge known to man." (If you have a piece of paper and pen, draw a pie shape within the circle that represents the remaining twenty percent).

The atheist at this point may see what you're up to and say: "I have the knowledge I need to determine there is no God." However, they do not know what the remaining twenty percent of the knowledge is. Hence, this person is not an Atheist, they are an Agnostic - one who does not know if there is a God, or is still searching.

If I ever meet a person who believes they are an atheist, I like to ask them, *Tell me about the God you don't believe in - I probably don't believe in him either.* The flimsiness of atheism is summed up in the quote by Luis Bunuel: "I'm still an atheist, thank God."

The Infinite Sovereignty of God

If we believe that God is in control of all things, we know He is overseeing that which is seemingly chaotic, and that which seems to be in order. If we are sure that we are unsure, or certain of uncertainty - we can view the uncertainty as creativity in process; knowing the disorder is happening in an orderly fashion. In example: A painting of an artist that is not yet complete, seems to be chaotic or uncertain, but to the artist, it is creativity in process.

The word "God", is a word symbol that encapsulates the limitlessness of the source of all things. The subsequent scriptural precedent, is the right of passage into the reality of the absolute sovereignty of the Creator of the Universe:

I Chronicles 29:11-12 Thine, O Lord, is greatness, and the power, and the glory, and the victory, and the majesty: for all that is in the heaven and in the earth is thine; thine is the kingdom, O Lord, and thou art exalted as head above all. Both riches and honour come of thee, and thou reignest over all.

Daniel 4:17 The most high rules in the kingdoms of men.

Proverbs 16:33 The lot is cast into the lap; but the whole disposing is of the Lord.

Psalm 8:6 Thou hast put all things under his feet.

Ecclesiastes 3:1 To everything there is a season, and a time to every purpose under heaven.

Matthew 28:18 All authority is given unto me in heaven and earth.

Romans 11:36 Out of Him and through Him and to Him are all things.

II Corinthians 5:18 All things are of God.

Ephesians 1:11 He works all things after the counsel of His will.

Colossians 1:17 He is before all things and in Him all things consist.

Hebrews 2:8 Thou hast put all things in subjection under his feet.

OUR OMNI GOD

Our Creator and the unconditional lover of our soul is the Infinite Center, who as the song says: "Holds the whole world in his hands." The only condition of receiving His unconditional love, is the condition of believing in it. Your God is:

OMNISCIENT: All Knowing.
OMNIPRESENT or OMNIEXISTENT: Present Everywhere.
OMNIPOTENT: Having All Power.
OMNIFICENT: Does All That is Done.

The Tree of the Knowledge of Good and Evil

Genesis 2:17 chronicles God telling Adam and Eve, they were not to eat from the Tree of the Knowledge of Good and Evil. If they did, they would be in sin. The sin was making a separation, or duality, between the Creator and the Creation - by saying: "This is God and this is not God." The highest plan of God for them, and You and I today, is to eat from the Tree of Life, knowing that all things are of God, both good and evil. Hamlet said: *There is nothing good or bad, but thinking makes it so. To me, it is a prison.*

Though we are not to eat from the Tree of the Knowledge of Good and Evil, we are to have our senses exercised to discern good and evil (Hebrews 5:14) so that, we may overcome evil with good (Romans 12:21). In our spiritual evolution on Earth, the Lord is moving us from insulated innocence into uninsulated innocence. We are to live as wise as a serpent and innocent as a dove (Matthew 10:16), knowing that - what we get, is what we are.

The thought naturally springs to mind: If God is Love, why is there evil? The answer is almost too simple for us, evil exists because - Nothing can exist without its opposite. If there was ever anything impossible for God, it would be to create something without its opposite. How can we know what good is, unless there was evil? We cannot know what is true, unless we also understand what is false. Wet defines dry; tall defines short; wide defines narrow; slow gives distinction to fast. Without polarities in the Universe, we would have no frame of reference.

No doubt, the preceding paragraph may be stepping on some deeply held beliefs. The prophet Isaiah wrote: I the Lord form the light and create darkness: I make peace and create evil, I the Lord do all these things (Isaiah 45:7).

Some have attempted to reframe this passage - by saying, "God allows evil." However, a simple study of the Hebrew word for "Create" - uncovers the word "Bara," which is the same Hebrew word used in Genesis 1:1, when God created the heavens and the earth. God did not allow the heavens and earth to come into being, He spoke them into existence.

To add depth and breadth to our understanding on this

issue, the following parallel scriptures will validate the truth of Isaiah 45:7, that God does indeed create evil. Stay mindful that Jesus warned the Pharisees and Scribes of attempting to neutralize the Word of God for the sake of their tradition (Mark 7:13).

1. Genesis 2:9 Out of the ground the Lord caused to grow the Tree of Life and the Tree of the Knowledge of Good and Evil.

2. Deuteronomy 30:15 I have set before you this day life and death...good and evil.

3. I Samuel 16:14 But the Spirit of the Lord departed from Saul, and an evil spirit from the Lord troubled him. (CF: I Samuel 18-10 and 19:9 say the same thing).

4. Job 1:21-22 The Lord gave, and the Lord hath taken away, blessed be the name of the Lord...in all this Job sinned not nor charged God foolishly.

5. Job 42:11 The Lord brought the evil on Job.

6. Proverbs 16:4 The Lord has made all things for himself; yea, even the wicked for the day of evil.

7. Ecclesiastes 1:10 I have seen the travail, which God hath given to the sons of men to be exercised in it.

8. Isaiah 13:6 Howl ye, for the day of the Lord is at hand, it shall come as a destruction from the Almighty.

9. Isaiah 13:10 Behold, the day of the Lord cometh both with wrath and fierce anger, to lay the land desolate: and to destroy the sinners thereof out of it.

10. Jeremiah 5:12 They have lied about the Lord saying, Evil shall not befall you.

11. Jeremiah 19:3 Thus saith the Lord God of host of Israel; Behold, I shall bring evil upon this place, the which whosoever heareth, his ears shall tingle.

12. Jeremiah 23:11-12 I shall bring evil upon the prophet and priest that are profane.

13. Jeremiah 23:16-17 Listen not to the false prophets that make you vain...they say no evil shall come upon you.

14. Jeremiah 24:10 And I will send the sword, the famine, and the pestilence among them until they are consumed.

15. Jeremiah 25:29 I shall bring evil upon the city called by my name, I'll call for the sword upon the earth.

16. Jeremiah 45:5 I shall bring evil upon all flesh saith the Lord.

17. Ezekiel 14:22 I shall bring evil upon Jerusalem.

18. Ezekiel 15:7 (Of Jerusalem) - They shall go out from one fire and another shall devour them.

19. Amos 9:4 I shall set my eyes against them for evil

and not good.

20. Amos 9:10 All the sinners of my people will die by the sword, those who say, Evil will not come upon us nor prevent us.

21. Micah 1:12 The inhabitants of Morah waited carefully for good: but evil came down from the Lord unto the gate of Jerusalem.

22. Micah 2:3 Behold, against this family do I devise an evil, from which ye shall never remove your necks.

23. Micah 3:11 (Of Israel) Her leaders judge for a bribe, priests teach for a price, prophets divine for money, Yet they lean on the Lord saying, The Lord is in our midst evil shall not come upon us.

24. Zephaniah 1:12 I'll search Jerusalem with candles and punish the men settled on their lees, who say in their hearts, The Lord shall neither do good nor will he do evil.

25. Malachi 4:6 Turn the heart of the fathers to the children, and the heart of the children to the fathers, lest I come and smite the earth with a curse.

26. Romans 1:8 The wrath of God is revealed from heaven. (How? The Law of Cause and Effect).

27. Galatians 6:7 Be not deceived, the Lord is not mocked, whatever a man sows that shall he also reap.

These scriptures can throw us out of concert with the way we have been brought up. Never forget - nothing can exist without it's opposite. All of the ways of God are based in love and are corrective in nature. The judgment of God always flows from his mercy and love to set us free from ourselves.

Hebrew Mysticism

During the course of my studies, my curiosity led me to explore the Jewish roots of my Christian faith. I became interested in the meaning of the twenty-two Hebrew letters which form every word of the Old Testament. On certain occasions, by understanding the original Hebrew word, we can receive a more lucid picture of the meaning of the text. Eventually, this led to reading and paging through various books on Jewish Mysticism, which naturally leads you into the Kabbalah. The entertainer Madonna, in recent years, has been sharing with the public her practice of the Kabbalah (or, Qabalah). The word Kabbalah simply means - revelation. It is a practical philosophy used by some for spiritual growth.

If you have studied this philosophy, you are aware of its central symbol, the Tree of Life, which includes the ten Sephiroth. Each Sephira represents a manifestation of the presence of God, which corresponds to a name of God:

Sefiroth	Experience	Name of God
Kether	Crown	Ehyeh Asher Ehyeh
Chockmah	Wisdom	Yah
Binah	Understanding	YHVH
Chesed	Love	El
Geburah	Strength	Elokim
Tiphareth	Beauty	YHVH

Netzach	Victory	Adonoy Tzevaot
Hod	Splendor	Elokim Tzevaot
Yesod	Foundation	Shaddai (El Chai)
Malkuth	Kingdom	Adonoy

Daath

Some teachers of the Kabbalah also mention Daath – the secret Sephira. This eleventh Sephira is supposedly the *"hidden and transcendental gateway of mystical perception – the esoteric corridor into supernatural consciousness"* through which we enter into the manifestation of the presence of God in the third dimension. If this is true, the key that unlocks the door of the secret knowledge of Daath, is simply believing that - Everything is happening for a reason. The reason is, by believing ETHFAR, you begin partaking of the Tree of Life (Genesis 2:9).

Just as Toto pulled back the curtain on the Wizard of Oz – this understanding yanks away the veil on every secret society which attempts to shroud themselves in the mysteries of the Hermetic sciences – who exploit the spiritual thirst of many seeking the truth, yet only provide them with a few innocuous drops of water.

Revelation 22:1 states: And he shewed me a pure river of water of life, clear as crystal, proceeding out of the throne of God and of the Lamb.

Revelation 22:17 announces: And the Spirit and the bride say, Come. And let him that heareth say, Come. And let him that is athirst come. And whosoever will, let him take the water of life freely.

35

Triangulations of the Trinity

Jesus loves you - and at times, enjoys making you smile or laugh by being playful with you. His love can be exhibited as a friend, sibling, parent, lover, or colleague. As you go through life knowing - Everything is happening for a reason; knowing that all things are of God, you will begin to appreciate the sense of humor of our infinite God. When you look up the word *triangulation* in the dictionary, or on the Internet, it usually has something to do with a math theorem.

However, there is a sociological definition of the word used at times by psychologists. To *triangulate* - is to communicate indirectly using juxtaposition. For instance, let's say a guy is driving along with his girlfriend who inspires him to believe he is the most fortunate guy on the planet. They pull up to a stoplight, next to them is his dream car. He might begin to triangulate his love or infatuation for her by saying something like – That car sure has nice lines, doesn't it honey?

In the last eight years, as I've implemented ETHFAR into my belief system, I have been riveted at times of the synchronicities that actualize between my thoughts, and what I might be watching on television, listening to on the radio, or even discussing with a friend or stranger. You will begin to notice these coincidences happening to you every day. They will be a sign, seal, and a wonder to you, of the universal monarchy of God. You will begin to think – Wow! - was that really God?

As time goes on, these little epiphanies will continue to reinforce your belief and faith in the All-Mighty. This will be a reminder that life is for our enjoyment: I Timothy 6:17b says: "Trust in the living God, who giveth us richly all things to enjoy." I especially appreciate the love of God being expressed to us through the beauty of nature and the playfulness of animals. There is no coincidence that the word *Dog*, is God, spelled backwards. The last few years I've begun to understand and love cats. Someone told me the difference between dogs and cats: Dogs think we are family – Cats think we are staff.

As a word of wisdom concerning the synchronicities that happen to us, it is important to not be led astray by these outward events, signs, or, symbols. Don't be seduced and reduced by outward appearances. The Lord wants us to be led strictly by faith in the Word of God and by the inner witness of the Holy Spirit:

Jonah 2:8 They that observe lying vanities forsake their own mercy.

II Corinthians 4:18 While we look not at he things which are seen, but at the things which are not seen: for the things which are seen are temporal; but the things which are not seen are eternal.

Colossians 3:15a Let the peace of God rule your hearts.

The Still Is The Master of the Restless

Angeles Arrian has written: *Worry is an interesting state of consciousness because it has us living in the past and fearing our future while completely avoiding the present.* There is much ado concerning Living In The Now, springing forth from self-help books these days. Eckhart Tolle's book *The Power of Now*, has been popular in some circles. The opening quote on his web-site states: To meet everything and everyone through stillness instead of mental noise is the greatest gift you can offer the universe.

To keep our mind peaceful in the present tense, requires

not eating from the Tree of the Knowledge of Good and Evil. Alternately, we then automatically begin to dine on the Tree of Life, knowing that all things are of God, that the external world is God's mirror reflection back to us – of what we have been sowing. If your present circumstances appear negative, to not embrace a guilty conscience, know that you are now bathed in the infinite and unconditional love of God.

Simultaneously, we must take ownership for our thoughts and actions, as we will reap what we sow. Through the Universal Law of Cause and Effect, we can feel confidently assured that the seeds we plant - will someday form our harvest. The time between the seed and the harvest - is when we grow in patience. Growth in patience always happens slowly.

THE FINE ART OF LIVING IN THE NOW

Once we have internally established that everything is happening for a reason, we can move forward in our new resolve by living our lives in Action Without Striving. This is the fundamental principle of Zen; Taoists call it *Wu wei*. Practically, this means: Planting seeds and not forcing the harvest, or, Saying little and saying it gently. Another way of putting it is: Living by the Golden Rule – Whatsoever ye would that men should do to you, do ye even so to them (Matthew 7:12) .

According to Angeles Arrien, the four principles in the Art of Living are:

1. Be on time.
2. Pay attention
3. Tell the Truth
4. Do not be attached to your agenda or an outcome.

The I-Ching (Book of Changes) was the Oracle of the Court of King Wen, who ruled the Chinese Zhou Dynasty over three thousand years ago. The I-Ching is the foundation of Lao Tzu's *Hua Hu Ching* and *Tao De Ching* (the second largest selling book in the world next to the Bible). It teaches us: To try and control people or circumstances is akin to trying to keep the earth from spinning, we exhaust our energy in vain.

King Solomon wrote: Trust in the Lord with all thine heart; and lean not unto thine own understanding. In all thy ways acknowledge him, and he shall direct thy path (Proverbs 3:5-6). The essence of Solomon's thought is echoed by the Apostles Paul and Timothy: Be anxious for nothing; but in everything by prayer and supplication with thanksgiving let your requests be made known unto to God. And the peace of God, which passes all understanding, shall keep your hearts and minds through Jesus Christ (Philippians 4:6-7).

When we place our trust in God, and conduct our affairs by the four principles listed above, we are on our way to bringing peace on the earth and goodwill to all men.

The Spirit of Radio
Album: Permanent Waves

Begin the day
With a friendly voice
A companion, unobtrusive
Plays that song that's so elusive
And the magic music makes your
morning mood

Off on your way
Hit the open road
There is magic at your fingers
For the Spirit ever lingers
Undemanding contact
In your happy solitude
Invisible airwaves
Crackle with life
Bright antennae bristle
With the energy
Emotional feedback
On a timeless wavelength
Bearing a gift beyond price –
Almost free…

All this machinery
Making modern music
Can still be open-hearted
Not so coldly charted
It's really just a question
Of your honesty
One likes to believe
In the freedom of music

But glittering prizes
And endless compromises
Shatter the illusion
Of integrity

"For the words of the profits,
Are written on the studio wall,
Concert hall -
Echoes with the sounds…
Of salesmen."

CHAPTER TWO

Freewill:

Do we meditate, or, are we being meditated?

Every explicit duality - is an implicit unity.
Alan Watts

There is no person on Earth who desires to be a robot or knowingly enslaved at the will of the whims of others. We all want to be individuals with a free spirit, soul, and body. If you were pointedly asked the question: Do you have freewill, yes or no? You would probably quickly respond – "Indeed, you better believe it! I have freewill."

Through further reflection, we might begin to question our freewill. In all reality, if our will is truly free, why is it that we cannot yet walk on water, or soar like an eagle through the canyons, or consume all the deep-dish barbeque chicken pizza we want, followed by a quart of pecan praline ice cream, without concerning ourselves with gaining weight?

Hence, do we have freewill or the impression of freewill?

An analogy that can aid us in understanding freewill, is that of prisoners in a cell. They have the ability to move around at will, but in the larger scheme of things, are not free to go out into society. Have you ever said to yourself or others during a time of being frustrated with life, "I never asked to be born!" If we truly had freewill, we would have been able to choose whether or not we wanted to be born into this world.

In 1929, Albert Einstein gave a rare interview in his Berlin apartment to an interviewer he had warmed up to named George Sylvester Viereck. After they ascended into the attic studio where the world-renowned mathematician peered into the mysteries of the universe, Viereck wasted no time. His first question to Einstein was: Do you believe man is a free agent? Einstein replied:

No, I am a determinist, compelled to act as if free will existed, because if I wish to live in a civilized society I must act responsibly. I know that philosophically a murderer is not responsible for his crime, but I prefer not to take tea with him. Undoubtedly my career has been determined by various factors over which I have no control, primarily those mysterious glands in which nature prepares the very essence of life. Henry Ford may call it his Inner Voice, Socrates referred to it as his daemon: each man explains in his own way the fact that the human will is not free…Everything is determined, the beginning as well as the end, by forces over which we have no control. It is determined for the insect as well as for the star. Human beings, vegetables, or cosmic dust, we all dance to a mysterious tune, intoned in the distance by an invisible player. (Einstein A Life; page 185; by Denis Brian; Published by John Wiley & Sons, Inc.)

What Is Going On

Imagine how God may have been thinking before the creation of Time and Space. God is infinity – there is no quality or quantity greater than God. So He says to Himself:

Well, here I am - with all this infinite expression. I have an idea: I will create visible expressions of myself - this way each expression (cell of awareness) can develop in never-ending creativity within Time and Space.

So here we are – six billion beings of light spread around the Earth, each on our own road of spiritual evolution. When we look out at the stars in the sky at night, they are a mirror reflection of all of us on Earth.

Each individual aspect of God (You and I) yearned for it's own expression – freewill. Subsequently, God divided Himself into billions of trinities - spirit, soul, and body, while still retaining infinite sovereignty as the Trinity of trinities. Quite the mystery indeed - maybe someday there will be trillions of trinities.

Groucho Marx remarked - Time is what keeps everything from happening at once.

The Urantia Book states - The simultaneous events within infinity are being presented as sequential transactions throughout eternity.

In a Biblical reframing of that thought we could add: The innumerable creative reactions of the Alpha and Omega (which are Yin and Yang in nature) are the simultaneous events of infinity (God) that are manifesting as sequential transactions throughout the endless horizons of eternity.

To keep it concise: Infinity is manifesting through Eternity.

Some assume Eternity and Infinity are one in the same. My position is this: Eternity is a quantity - the continuum of Time and Space. Infinity is a quality - the presence of God = The Spirit. Isaiah 57:15 says – "God inhabits eternity." So then, infinity also exists within eternity. To make the mystical - practical, this means: Everything that God has planned, is going to be done within Time and Space.

Eternity is a straight line. Infinity is a circle – or, a continually expanding sphere with an endless core in which new waves of creativity will keep unfolding throughout time everlasting. It is archived in Ephesians 2:7 - "That in the ages to come (Time and Space) he might show the exceeding riches of his grace in his kindness toward us through Jesus Christ."

The Imperial Paradigm

When balancing Joshua 24:15 "Choose you this day whom you will serve," with Ephesians 1:11 "God works all things after the counsel of his own will," – we are left with a new paradigm in understanding who we are. This equilibrium can be summed up in the phrase:

We are all visible expressions of the Invisible.

This is an echo of Genesis 1:26 where it is chronicled that we were created in the image and likeness of God. Around the age of nine, I recall carrying some groceries to the pantry for my mother. Just before I opened the door, I remember this thought dropping into my mind: Everyone is one drop of God's personality.

This was the first time in my life I consciously knew that God had communicated something to me. Some people become cynical, and say - it concerns them when they hear people say they heard from God. How concerned are they? What's worse is - when people don't hear from God. Over the years, the afterimage of that thought I had while carrying the groceries, has crystallized itself into the following assertions:

We are images of the Imageless.

We are forms of the Formless.

The third and fourth dimensions are one = The natural world and spiritual world are one.

The visible and invisible are one = The Music of the Spheres.

The Creation is an expression of the Creator.

Eastern mystical circles speak of - The One - that we are all connected to a divine source. Even though I believe this is true, for me, speaking of God as The One seems to me, nondescript and nebulous, projecting an impersonal presence to the loving Creator of the universe. The One - is known more personally in the Hebrew language as Elohim. Jesus rocks the foundation of our traditional tendencies in John 10:34 when he declares: "Is it not written in your law, I said, Ye are gods?" Jesus was reflecting on Psalm 82:6 "I have said, Ye are gods; and all of you are children of the most High."

The Hebrew word for - gods, in English is - Elohim. An apple tree produces apple seeds; an orange tree produces orange seeds. Since we are the offspring of God, or His seed, we are gods. Personally, I don't need to go through life thinking of myself as a god. However, the Lord does want us to reign in life over things of the darkness. The last portion of I John 4:17 should thrill us: As he is, so are we in this world.

Our Pre-Existence

The one question that always loses me in wonder, and sometimes frustration is: How can God have always existed? Perhaps someday when we are free from mortal darkness, we will comprehend the answer. The answer will have nothing to do with time and space, but a clear sensation of what timelessness is - moving beyond the division of Time, into the singularity of Timelessness. Beyond the duality of Taoism, into the singularity of Nowism.

Another question that sets the wheels of our mind in motion is: Can non-existence - exist?

Could our non-existence, have ever existed? Did we pre-exist before we were born? The following passages reveal that we did exist in God before we came into Earth:

Job 38:4 (God asks Job) Where wast thou when I laid the foundations of the earth? Declare if thou hast understanding. When the morning stars sang together, and all the sons of God shouted for joy.

God did not ask Job if he was there, but if he had understanding of being there when the foundations of the earth were being fashioned. Jesus is the Bright and Morning Star - we were one with God before He created Himself into billions of visible expressions.

Psalm 8:4-5 What is man, that thou are mindful of him? And the son of man, that thou visitest him? For thou hast made him a little lower than the angels.

The word - angels, in the previous verse - is the Hebrew word "Elohim," which is normally translated –God, in the Old Testament. Evidently, the translators did not comprehend what they were translating. In Young's Literal Translation of the Bible, this verse reads, "Thou causest him (mankind) to lack a little of the Godhead." Hence, before humanity was brought into being, we were one with God. Now we are one with God, as an innumerable body of individual third dimensional expressions.

Psalm 22:27 All the ends of the world shall remember and turn unto the Lord: and all the kindreds of the nations shall worship before thee.

What is it that we will remember? We shall one day have recollection that we were once one with God in pure spirit form.

Psalm 90:1-3 Lord, thou hast been our dwelling place in all generations. Before the mountains were brought forth, or ever thou hast formed the earth and the world, even from everlasting to everlasting thou art God. Thou turnest man to destruction and sayest, Return ye children of men.

Ecclesiastes 12:7 Then shall the dust return to the earth as it was: and the spirit shall return to God who gave it.

We could not understand what "returning" to God means, unless we were already with God in spirit form before our earthly existence. We cannot "return" to a foreign country that we have not yet been to.

Jeremiah 1:5 Before I formed thee in the belly I knew thee; and before thou camest forth out of the womb I sanctified thee, and I ordained thee a prophet unto the nations

Romans 8:20-21 For the creation was subjected to futility, not of it's own will, but because of him who subjected it in hope that the creation itself also will be set free from it's slavery to corruption into the freedom of the glory of the children of God.

If you have ever had the thought: "I never asked to be born" - you are right. As a continuative to that thought, the previous verse implies that we were unwilling to be born into the Earth - subjected or lowered from the realm of spirit into this material world.

What the Bible says concerning Freewill

For those that believe the Bible is the final authority on freewill, the following scriptures solidify the reality that God is indeed, the Sovereign All in All:

Daniel 4:17 This matter is by decree of the watchers, and the demand by the word of the holy ones: to the intent that the living may know that the most High ruleth in the kingdoms of men, and giveth it to whomsoever he will, and setteth up over it the basest of men.

Daniel 4:35 He doeth according to his will in the army of heaven, and among the inhabitants of the earth: and none can stay his hand, or say unto him, What doest thou?

John 1:13 (Of believers) - Which were born, not of blood, nor the will of the flesh, nor the will of man, but of God.

John 5:21 The Son quickeneth whom he will.

John 6:44 (Jesus said) No man can come to me (by his own will) except the Father which hath sent me, draws him.

John 15:16 Ye have not chosen me, but I have chosen you.

Romans 9:16 So then it is not of him that willeth, nor of him that runneth, but of God that sheweth mercy.

Romans 9:19 Who has resisted his will? (Note: All

of chapter nine and eleven in the Book of Romans are excellent in determining the sovereignty of God).

Ephesians 1:11 God worketh all things after the counsel of His will.

Ephesians 2:8-9 For by grace are you saved through faith; and that is not of yourselves (not of your will): it is the gift of God: not of works lest any man should boast

Revelation 17:17 For God hath put in their hearts to fulfill his will.

The Infinite Fine Line

Over the years when discussing the title of my book with friends and family, I've told them it is based in Ephesians 1:11 "God works all things after the counsel of his own will." From the moment in the summer of 1996 when I grabbed onto the thought - Everything Is Happening For A Reason, and began repeating it to myself throughout the coming weeks and years, that scripture was the anchor for my heart and mind to believe this adage to be an absolute. The sovereignty of God, when viewed in the context of ETHFAR, is so huge, so grand, so infinite (How infinite is that!), it can only be understood by faith.

Someone has said: "If faith is blind - through darkness it will guide us." In my own useless struggle in trying to fathom the mystery of Freewill within the intellectual sense - I have resigned myself to enjoy the mystery. The mystery that God is in control of all things - down to the infinite nth of every second of every day, versus the will of man being done, is the timeless mystery I call The Infinite Fine Line.

A Farewell to Kings
Album: A Farewell to Kings

When they turn the pages of history
When these days have passed long ago
Will they read of us with sadness
For the seeds that we let grow
We turned our gaze
From the castles in the distance
Eyes cast down
On the path of least resistance

Cities full of hatred
Fear and lies
Withered hearts
And cruel, tormented eyes
Scheming demons
Dressed in kingly guise
Beating down the multitude
And scoffing at the wise

The hypocrites are slandering
The sacred halls of Truth
Ancient nobles showering
Their bitterness on youth
Can't we find
The minds that made us strong
Can't we learn
To feel what's right and wrong

Cities full of hatred
Fear and lies
Withered hearts
And cruel, tormented eyes
Scheming demons
Dressed in kingly guise
Beating down the multitude
And scoffing at the wise
Can't we raise our eyes
And make a start
Can't we find the minds
To lead us closer to the Heart

CHAPTER THREE

The Restoration of All Things

Do you imagine the universe is agitated?
Go into the desert at night and look out at the stars.
Brian Browne Walker

In the light of what has been established of the love and sovereignty of God, it would be contradictory to believe in the eternal damnation teachings that have been leveraged against humanity since the fourth century. Since the Alpha and Omega is in control of all things, this would presuppose He has been creating people, knowing He would ultimately be damning some to endless torture - this is pure fallacy. The sweet consistency in believing in the salvation of all people, is that it coincides with the promise made to Abraham: "In thy seed shall all people of the earth be blessed." In addition, it amplifies the unlimited majesty of Jesus Christ who has all power in heaven and earth.

Jesus Christ came as a teacher, prophet, and the Messiah of the Abrahamic Covenant. The term – "Restitution of all things" appears in Acts 3:19-26 where it also foretells of the times of refreshing and the fulfillment of the Abrahamic Covenant. Nowhere in the Bible does it speak of the - Restoration of some things. Jesus did not say - Behold, I make some things new (Revelation 21:5). When God says - All, He means All.

The History of Apokatastasis

Apokatastasis is the Greek word for Restitution found in Acts 3:21. The 1908 edition of *The Schaff–Herzog Encyclopedia of Religious Knowledge* (Volume 12; page 96) provides a glimpse into the extent that Apokatastasis was taught in the post–apostolic era of Christianity:

> In the first five or six centuries of Christianity, there were six known theological schools, of which four (Alexandria, Antioch, Caesarea, and Edessa) were Universalist, one (Ephesus) accepted conditional immortality; one (Carthage or Rome) taught endless punishment for the wicked.

The New Schaff-Herzog Encyclopedia of Religious Knowledge (Vol. 12; page 96) states:

> Under the instruction of those great teachers many other theologians believed in universal salvation; and indeed the whole Eastern Church until after 500 A.D. was inclined to it.

The following church leaders of the post-Apostolic period, were Christian Universalists -all believed in and proclaimed the Restoration of All Things:

Clement of Alexandria
Origen
Theophilus: Bishop of Antioch
Athenagoras
Pamphilus
Eusebius: Bishop of Caesarea and first church historian.
Gregory of Nazianzus
Gregory of Nyssa
Ambrose: Bishop of Milan

Of these men, Origen (185-254) was the most well-known. The popularity of his teaching on The Restoration of All Things (Apokatastasis) was so wide-spread, and such a threat to the Roman Empire, that the Emperor Justinian and his Empress Theadora, suffering from a heightened sense of anxiety, had him excommunicated at the Fifth Ecumenical Council of the Catholic Church (553 A.D.).

This was 300 years after Origen was dead - he probably didn't lose any sleep over it. Even Pope Vigilius, who presided over the Roman Catholic Church at the time, refused to ratify the declaration against Origen. However, in this instance, the big money had their way - Pope Vigilius was forced to concede to their edict. Uneventfully, Pope Vigilius mysteriously died on the road home to Rome.

Interestingly, many of the Founding Fathers of the United States were Christian Universalists:

John Adams
John Quincy Adams
Ethan Allen
Benjamin Franklin
Thomas Jefferson
James Madison
Thomas Paine
Paul Revere

Other well-known individuals that have been Christian Universalists are:

Charles Dickens (Author)
Ralph Waldo Emerson (Author)
Nathaniel Hawthorne (Author)
Henry David Thoreau (Poet, Author)
Oliver Wendell Holmes (Justice of US Supreme Court)
Herman Melville (Author)
Susan B. Anthony (Activist in antislavery movement)
Clara Barton (Founder of American Red Cross)
Frank Lloyd Wright (Architect)
Alexander Graham Bell (Invented Telephone, founded National Geographic magazine)
Samuel Morse (Artist, Invented Telegraph)
Isaac Newton (Mathematician, Scientist)
Henry Longfellow (Poet)

By the time you have finished this chapter, you will discover that the following Biblical Patriarchs were also Universalists:

Moses
Abraham
King David
King Solomon
The prophet Isaiah
The prophet Jeremiah
The prophet Ezekiel
The prophet Daniel
The prophet Hosea
The prophet Joel
The prophet Micah
Jesus Christ – The King of kings.
The Apostle Paul

The Apostle Timothy
The Apostle Peter
The Apostle John

Overwhelming Evidence

The following passages of Holy Scripture solidify the belief of The Restoration of All Things. Most are paraphrased for expediency - please take time to read them in their full context. For any that believe that I have taken any of the following scriptures out of context, please focus on the ones that you believe are not out of context. Of the ninety-seven scriptures that are provided, if only two of them are relevant - The Restoration of All Things (The Gospel) should be seriously discussed in the churches around the world from now on.

Old Testament Precedent for The Restoration of All Things:

1. Genesis 12:3 All families of the earth shall be blessed.

2. Genesis 13:16 I will make thy seed as the dust of the earth: so if a man can number the dust of the earth, then shall thy seed also be numbered.

3. Genesis 15:5 If thou be able to number the stars, So shall thy seed be.

4. Genesis 18:18 All the nations of the earth shall be blessed in him.

5. Genesis 22:18 In thy seed shall all the nations of the

earth be blessed.

6. Genesis 26:4 Thy seed shall multiply as the stars of heaven, and all nations shall be blessed.

7. Genesis 28:14 Thy seed shall be as the dust of the earth, all families of the earth shall be blessed.

8. I Samuel 2:6 The Lord kills, and makes alive what he brings down to the grave, and brings up.

9. Job 12:9-10 In the hand of the Lord is the soul of every living thing, and the breath of all mankind.

10. I Chronicles 27:23 David knew the Lord would increase Israel like the stars of the heavens. (This is a powerful scripture: David knew that all people would eventually become God's People=Israel)

11. Psalms 2:7-8 Thou art my Son; this day have I begotten thee, I shall give thee the heathen for thine inheritance, and the uttermost parts of the earth for thy possession.

12. Psalm 8:6 Thou hast made him to have dominion over the works of thy hands; thou hast put all things under his feet.

13. Psalm 22:27 All the ends of the world shall remember and turn unto the Lord: and all the kindreds of the nations shall worship before thee.

14. Psalm 24:1 The earth is the Lord's and the fullness thereof; the world, and they that dwell therein.

15. Psalms 65: 2 and 5 O thou that hearest prayer, unto thee shall all flesh come. Thou art the confidence of all the ends of the earth, and of them that are afar off upon the sea.

16. Psalms 66:3-4 Through the greatness of thy power shall thine enemies submit themselves unto thee. All the earth shall worship thee, and shall sing unto thee; they shall sing to thy name.

17. Psalm 67:7 God shall bless us; and all the ends of the earth shall fear him.

18. Psalm 68:18 God has led the rebellious into captivity that He might dwell among them.

19. Psalm 72:17 (King David's last Psalm) His name shall endure forever: his name shall be continued as long as the sun: and men shall be blessed in him: all nations shall call him blessed.

20. Psalm 82:8 Arise, O God, judge the earth: for thou shalt inherit all nations.

21. Psalm 86:9 All nations whom thou hast made shall come and worship before thee, O Lord ;and shall glorify thy name.

22. Psalm 90:3 Thou turnest man to destruction; and sayest, Return, ye children of men.

23. Psalm 138:4 All the kings of the earth shall praise thee.

24. Psalms 145:9-10 The Lord is good to all: and his tender mercies are over all his works. All thy works

shall praise thee, O Lord, and thy saints shall bless thee.

25. Isaiah 2:2 All nations shall flow unto the house of the Lord.

26. Isaiah 11:9 The earth shall be full of the knowledge of the Lord as the waters cover the sea.

27. Isaiah 14:24 The Lord of hosts has sworn, saying, Surely as I have thought, so shall it come to pass; and as I have purposed, so shall it stand.

28. Isaiah 19:25 The Lord shall bless Egypt his people, Assyria the work of his hands, and Israel his inheritance.

29. Isaiah 25:6-8 In the mountain of the Lord shall all people feast on fat things. He will destroy the face of the covering cast over all people. He will wipe away tears from off all faces.

30. Isaiah 45:22-23 Look unto me, and be ye saved, all the ends of the earth: for I am God, and there is none else. Unto me every knee shall bow and every tongue shall swear.

31. Isaiah 46:10 Declaring the end from the beginning, and from ancient times the things that are not yet done, saying, My counsel shall stand, and I will do all my pleasure. (Note: Based on Ephesians 1:10, we know that it is God's pleasure that all people be one with him)

32. Isaiah 52:10 All the ends of the earth shall see the

salvation of our God. (The Hebrew word for *see* in this verse is *raah* which means, to experience)

33. Isaiah 66:23 All flesh shall come and worship before me, saith the Lord.

34. Jeremiah 3:17 All nations shall be gathered unto the throne of the Lord: they shall not walk after the imagination of their evil heart.

35. Jeremiah 4:2 The nations shall bless themselves in Him, and in Him shall they glory.

36. Ezekiel 16:55 When Sodom and Samaria are returned to their former state, then shall Jerusalem be returned to her former state. (Please read this whole chapter)

37. Daniel 4:1 Nebuchadnezzar declared, Peace be multiplied unto all people, nations, and languages, that dwell on the earth. (Directly after he saw the Lord rescue Shadrach, Meshach, and Abednego from the flaming furnace.)

38. Daniel 7:27 All dominions shall serve Him.

39. Hosea 1:10 It shall come to pass that in the place where it was said, You are not my people, it shall be said, You are the sons of the living God. (CF: Hosea 3:22-23)

40. Joel 2:28 I shall pour out my spirit upon all flesh.

41. Joel 3:21 I shall cleanse their blood that I have not cleansed: for the Lord dwells in Zion.

42. Micah 4:4 Every man shall sit under his own vine and fig tree and none shall make him afraid.

43. Micah 7:20 Thou wilt perform the truth to Jacob, and the mercy to Abraham, which thou hast sworn unto our fathers from the days of old. (No doubt this concerns the Abrahamic Covenant; that all peoples of the earth shall be blessed).

New Testament Precedent for The Restoration of All Things

1. Matthew 11:27 All things are delivered to me of my Father.

2. Matthew 17:11 Elijah shall come and restore all things. (He did in the sense that he prepared the way in the wilderness in declaring that Jesus was the Messiah).

3. Luke 2:10 And the angel said unto them, Fear not: for behold, I bring you good tidings of great joy, which shall be to all people.

4. Luke 3:6 All flesh shall see the salvation of God.

5. Luke 20:38 For he is not a God of the dead, but of the living: for all live unto him.

6. John 1:9 The true Light which lighteth every man that cometh into the world.

7. John 1:29 Behold, the Lamb of God, which taketh away the sin of the world.

8. John 3:17 God sent his Son that the world would be saved through him. (Will Jesus fail?)

9. John 4:42 Jesus is the Saviour of the world. (It does not say, the Saviour to the world).

10. John 6:39 This is the Fathers will, that of all which he hath given me I should lose nothing. (The question must be asked: Has Jesus failed the Heavenly Father?)

11. John 8:29 I always do those things that please Him. (This is the answer of Jesus to the previous question).

12. John 12:32 If I be lifted up, I shall draw all men unto me.

13. John 13:3 Jesus knew that the Father had given all things into his hands.

14. John 17:2 Thou hast given him power over all flesh, that he should give eternal life to as many as thou hast given him. (We know from Matthew 11:27 and John 13:3 that Jesus has been given all things from the Father).

15. John 17:23 God loves the world the same as he loves Jesus.

16. John 18:9 Of them which thou gavest me have I lost none (re-read John 6:39).

17. Acts 2:16-17 The spirit shall be poured out upon all flesh.

18. Acts 3:21 Heaven must receive Jesus until the times of restitution of all things, which God hath spoken by the mouth of all his holy prophets since the world began.

19. Acts 17:26 and 31 He hath made of one blood all nations of men for to dwell on all the face of the earth, and hath determined the times before appointed , and the bounds of their habitation. He hath given assurance unto all men.

20. Romans 5:18 Therefore as by the offence of one judgment came upon all men to condemnation; even so by the righteousness of one, the free gift came upon all men unto justification.

21. Romans 8:21 The creation itself also shall be delivered from bondage of corruption into the glorious liberty of the children of God.

22. Romans 9:16 So then it is not of him that willeth, nor of him that runneth, but of God that showeth mercy.

23. Romans 11:25-26 Blindness in part has happened to Israel, until the fullness of the Gentiles come in. And so all Israel shall be saved.

24. Romans 11:32 and 36 God hath concluded them all in unbelief, that he might have mercy upon them all. For of him, and through him, and to him, are all things.

25. I Corinthians 13:8 Love never fails. (Since God is Love (I John 4:8,16) it is reasonable to assume that God will not fail in actualizing His dream to save

everyone He has created).

26. I Corinthians 15: 22 and 28 For as in Adam all die, <u>even so</u> in Christ shall all be made alive. When all things shall be subdued unto him, then shall the Son himself be subjected unto him that put all things under him, that God may be all in all.

27. I Corinthians 15:47 *The first man is of the earth. The second man is the Lord from heaven.* This seemingly simple verse is packed with power to nail down with endless absolution the restoration of all things: All men died in Adam, who was the First Man (verse 45). All men are made alive in the Second Man, who was the Last Adam. According to Ephesians 2:15-16, Jesus crucified the First Man on the cross and was raised as the Second Man. All people that have ever been created exist in these two men. Since Jesus was crucified as the First Man on the cross, the only man left is the Second Man. Hence, all people exist in the Second Man. This is how we understand that God is All in All. Once we move beyond the simplicity of this verse, things get complicated.

28. II Corinthians 5:19 God was in Christ, reconciling the world unto himself, not imputing their trespasses against them; and hath committed unto us the word of reconciliation.

29. Galatians 3:8 The scripture foreseeing that God would justify the heathen through faith, preached the gospel unto Abraham, saying, In thee shall all nations be blessed.

30. Ephesians 1:10 In the dispensation of the fullness of

times he might gather together into one all things in Christ, both which are in heaven, and which are on earth; even in him.

31. Ephesians 1:21-23 God hath put all things under his feet, and gave him to be the head over all things to the church, which is his body, the fullness of him that filleth all in all.

32. Ephesians 4:6 There is one God and Father of all, who is above all, and through all, and in you all.

33. Philippians 2:10-11 At the name of Jesus every knee should bow, of things in heaven, and things in earth, and things under the earth; And that every tongue should confess that Jesus Christ is Lord, to the glory of God the Father.

34. Philippians 3:21 He is able to subdue all things unto himself.

35. Colossians 1:16,17 and 20 For by him were all things created, that are in heaven, and that are in earth, visible and invisible, whether they be thrones, or dominions, or principalities, or powers: all things were created by him, and for him: And he is before all things, and by him all things consist. And having made peace through the blood of his cross, by him to reconcile all things unto himself; by him, I say whether they be things in earth, or things in heaven.

36. Colossians 3:11 There is neither Greek nor Jew, circumcision nor uncircumcision, Barbarian, Scythian, bond nor free: but Christ is all, and in all.

37. I Timothy 2:4-6 God will have all men to be saved, and to come unto the knowledge of the truth. For there is one God, and one mediator between God and men, the man Christ Jesus; Who gave himself a ransom for all, to be testified in due time.

38. I Timothy 4:10-11 Trust in the living God, who is the Saviour of all men, especially of those that believe. These things command and teach.

39. Titus 2:11 For the grace of God that bringeth salvation hath appeared to all men.

40. Hebrews 1:2 God hath appointed his Son heir of all things, by whom also he made the worlds. (This is the fulfillment of the prophecy concerning Jesus in Psalm 2:7-8)

41. Hebrews 2:8 Thou hast put all things in subjection under his feet. For in that he put all in subjection under him, he left nothing that is not put under him. But now we see not yet all things put under him.

42. Hebrews 8:11 The time shall come when they will not teach every man his neighbor, and every man his brother, saying, Know the Lord: for all shall know me, from the least to the greatest.

43. James 1:18 Of his own will begat he us with the word or truth, that we should be a kind of firstfruits of his creatures.

44. James 2:13 Mercy rejoices against (triumphs over) judgment.

45. James 5:11 The end of the Lord is tender mercy. (Not a vengeful dictator looking to punish people for eternity)

46. I John 2:2 Jesus is the propitiation for our sins and for the sins of the whole world.

47. I John 4:14 We have seen and do testify that the Father sent the Son to be the Saviour of the world.

48. Revelation 4:11 Thou hast created all things, and for thy pleasure they are and were created.

49. Revelation 5:13 Every creature which is in heaven, and on earth, and under the earth, and such as are in the sea, <u>and all that are in them</u>, heard I saying, Blessing and honour, and glory, and power be unto him that sitteth upon the throne, and unto the Lamb for ever and ever.

50. Revelation 7: 9-10 And I beheld a great multitude, which no man could number, of all nations, and kindreds, and people, and tongues, stood before the Lamb, clothed with white robes, and palms in their hands; And cried with a loud voice, saying, Salvation to our God which sitteth upon the throne and unto the Lamb.

51. Revelation 11:15 The kingdoms of this world are become the kingdoms of our Lord and of his Christ.

52. Revelation 15:4 For all nations shall come and worship before thee; for thy judgments are made manifest.

53. Revelation 21:5 Behold, I make all things new. And he said unto me, Write: for these words are true and faithful (Jesus did not say, Behold, I make all new things).

54. Revelation 22:2-3 The tree of life shall bear fruit every month and the leaves of the tree were for the healing of the nations.

Does God Ever Call People - Things?

Inevitably, when the phrase – The Restoration of All Things, comes into play, we may find ourselves broaching the question: Does the Bible ever refer to people as things? The following passages support this notion:

1. Psalm 8:6 Thou hast put all things under his feet.

2. Proverbs 16:4 The Lord hath made all things for himself: yea, even the wicked for the day of evil.

3. Luke 1:35 That holy thing which shall be born of thee shall be called the Son of God. (If Jesus is willing to be called a *thing*, it's ok with me).

4. John 1:3 All things were made by him; and without him was not any thing made that was made.

5. I Corinthians 3:21-22 Therefore let no man glory in men. For all things are yours; whether Paul, or Apollos, or Cephas, or the world, or life, or death, or things present, or things to come; all are yours.

6. I Corinthians 15:28 When all things shall be subdued unto him, then shall the Son also himself be subjected unto him that put all things under him that

God may be all in all.

7. Philippians 2:10 At the name of Jesus every knee should bow, of things in heaven, and things in earth, and things under the earth.

8. Colossians 1:16 For by him were all things created, that are in heaven, in the earth, visible and invisible, whether they be thrones or dominions, or principalities, or powers: all things were created by him and for him.

9. Hebrews 1:2 Jesus has been appointed heir of all things.

10. Hebrews 2: 8 Thou hast put all things in subjection under his feet.

11. Hebrews 4:13 Neither is there any creature that is not manifest in his sight but all things are naked and opened unto the eyes of him with whom we have to do.

12. Revelation 4:11 Thou hast created all things, and for thy pleasure they were created.

13. Revelation 21:5 Behold, I make all things new.

Any church, ministry, televangelist, or, religious organizations which are disinclined to teaching or believing anything other than the Restoration of All Things, which is the fulfillment of the Abrahamic Covenant, they are teaching and believing, *another Jesus, another spirit, and another gospel* (II Corinthians 11:4). The Bible warns us of these types of ministries:

Ezekiel 5:6 And she hath changed my judgments into wickedness more than the nations.

II Peter 2:1 But there were false prophets also among the people, even as there shall be false teachers among you, who privily shall bring in damnable heresies (the Greek says "heresies of damnation") even denying the Lord that bought them, and bring upon themselves swift destruction.

I Timothy 4:1 Now the Spirit speaketh expressly, that in the latter times some shall depart from the faith, giving heed to seducing spirits and doctrines of devils.

There are many ministries out there warning us of false doctrines - when they themselves are teaching false doctrines. There is no doubt the thoughtless will announce their thoughtlessness. They will say: The Restoration of All Things message is of the Devil. My response is: For crying out loud, what sounds more devilish – God restoring all things unto Himself, or, that billions of people will roast in seething flames for eternity?
Hello.

God Will Save Unbelievers That Have Died

Nowhere in the Old or New Testament does it say that God will not save people after they have died. Nowhere. The unconditional love of God is not limited to the beating of the heart. Alternately, I Peter 4:6 proclaims:
For this cause was the gospel preached also to them that are dead, THAT they might be judged according

to men in the flesh, but live according to God in the spirit.

This passage of truth rattles the traditional mind.

For more scriptural back-up on this issue, take the time to consider the following scriptures in the light of the Restoration of All Things: I Samuel 2:6, Isaiah 24:22, Isaiah 42:7, Isaiah 61:1, Zechariah 9:11, Psalm 68:18, Ephesians 1:10, Ephesians 4:8-10, Philippians 2:10-11, I Peter 3:18-20.

You may wonder, If everyone is going to be saved, why should we serve God?

This is a question that you must answer yourself. For my answer, keep reading the rest of this book.

Turn The Page
Album: Hold Your Fire

Nothing can survive in a vacuum
No one can exist all alone
We pretend things
Only happen to strangers
We've all got problems of our own

It's enough to learn
To share our pleasures
We can't soothe pain with sympathy
All that we can do is be reminded-
We shake our heads at the tragedy

Every day we're standing
In a time capsule
Racing down a river from the past
Every day we're standing
In a wind tunnel
Facing down the future coming fast

It's just the age
It's just a stage-
We disengage-
We turn the page...

Looking at
The long-range forecast
Catching all the names in the news
Checking out
The state of the nation
Learning the environmental blues

Truth is after all a moving target
Hairs to split,
And pieces that don't fit
How can anybody be enlightened?
Truth is after all so poorly lit

CHAPTER FOUR

The Aionios Symposium

The Sun is only a shadow of a higher reality.
- Michael Alexander

Most people will agree the Bible has been mistranslated in certain areas, that we need to search out the Greek and Hebrew texts to decipher what certain words mean. In my estimation, the most reckless mistranslation in the Bible has been the Greek word Aionios, along with its various derivations. This Greek word has been translated to the word - Eternal, in most Bibles, when it should have been translated to - Of the Ages. The blatant mistranslation of this word in the New Testament, is the axis on which the illusion of Eternal Damnation spins - from the small town church on the corner, throughout suburbia and the metropolitan areas, to the national and international religious satellite networks.

You do not need to have a Doctorate in Greek to understand this chapter. Once the accuracy of this chapter is verified by your own due diligence, the myth of eternal damnation begins to come unglued. This chapter is the Rosetta stone to decode the intention of God for the Ages the golden key that unlocks the door into accepting the Restoration of All Things - the fulfillment of the Abrahamic Covenant (Acts 3:19-26).

If you were to write a letter to someone you knew who spoke only a foreign language (which you did not speak), they would need your letter translated into their own language. As a consequence, the original intent of your words may be lost in the translation. This holds true with Bible translations.

The Original Manuscripts of the Bible were inspired, translations are not. The following portion of this chapter comes from a portion of my notes scribbled down over the years, which convinced me that Eternal Damnation is an illusion. I did not believe in the Restoration of All Things overnight - it took four years of burning the midnight-oil before my reality shifted from being a Damnationist to a Restorationist.

The Seven Main Ages in the Bible

1. The Age of Innocence: The dawn of civilization starting with Adam and Eve before they ate from the Tree of the Knowledge of Good and Evil.

2. The Age of Conscience: After humanity had their eyes open to good and evil.

3. The Age of Promise: Promises made to Noah and Abraham.

4. The Age of Human Government: Before God set up Saul to rule over Israel, each man did what was right

in his own sight (Judges 21:25).

5. Age of Law: From Moses to Jesus.

6. The Church Age: From the disciples until now.

7. The Kingdom Age: Ephesians 1:10 speaks of - "The dispensation of the fullness of times, when all things shall be gathered together in Christ." This age is called the *Age of the Ages* in the Greek text of Ephesians 3:21.

Cracking the Code

Big doors swing on small hinges. The small hinge that shall transform your belief system in the Bible forever, giving you a new and fresh appreciation for the love of God and His plan for all people, is the Greek word Aion. The Latin counterpart Aeon, is where we arrive with the English word Eon, which simply means, an Age. The two main derivations of Aion in the New Testament, that have been horrifically mistranslated to the English word Eternal, are the Greek words Aionion (the plural of Aion) and Aionios (the adjective of Aion).

These translational inconsistencies, which disastrously eclipse the truth, leave us laughing at the dreadfulness of the scholastics of the translators. Hopefully, this will affect your opinion of their ability to effectively administer the word of God, in turn, spurring you on to – "study to show yourself approved" (II Timothy 2:15).

79

Matthew 25:46

"And these shall go away into everlasting punishment: but the righteous into life eternal."

The passage of the Sheep and Goats is probably the most popular Eternal Damnation passage in the Bible. In the first place, the Sheep and Goats narrative, is not about believers and unbelievers. We are not saved by works (Ephesians 2:8-9). The concept of the righteous and unrighteous, in this context, speaks of how compassionate we are towards humanity - the righteous and unrighteous works we do. Those that teach Eternal Damnation from this passage have been scripturally negligent - missing the point.

Both words - Everlasting and Eternal, in Matthew 25:46 are the Greek word Aionios, which means - the Ages. In the King James Version of the Bible, the phrase - eternal life or life eternal, is used thirty times in the New Testament. While the phrase, everlasting life, is used 14 times. Each time, the Greek word is Aionios - the adjective of Aion. The most intelligent way to interpret the Bible is with the Bible. To prove that Aionios does not mean - Endless, the following three passages unearth instances where translators were forced to use the word - *world*, instead of the words - *eternal* or *everlasting*, because it would sound wrong.

Romans 16:25 Now to him that is of power to stablish you according to my gospel, and the preaching of Jesus Christ, according to the revelation of the mystery, which was kept secret since the <u>world</u> (Aionios) began.

II Timothy 1:9b According to his own purpose and grace, which was given us in Christ Jesus before the <u>world</u> (Aionios) began.

Titus 1:2 In hope of eternal (Aionios) life, which God, that cannot lie, promised before the <u>world</u> (Aionios) began.

The verse in Titus is the most horrific - Aionios appears twice, the translators used two different words to describe it! In all three passages, the translators placed the word –*world*, on the Greek word - Aionios. We can't say – Since the eternal began. However, we can understand the phrase, Since the ages began.

Hebrews 1:2b says God – "Hath in these last days spoken unto us by his Son, whom he hath appointed heir of all things, by whom also he made the worlds (Ages)." God has created Time and Space (Genesis 1:-1-20), and through the endless horizons of eternity, shall pour out his blessing on us in Christ Jesus.

Zoë Aionios = The Life of the Ages

All serious students of the Bible, should have access to an Interlinear Bible. It shows us how the words of the original manuscripts were written down. Everytime I have checked the phrases listed in the left-hand column below in my Interlinear New Testament, they were written in the Greek as - Zoë Aionios, which means - The Life of the Ages:

<u>Incorrect Translation</u>	<u>Greek</u>	<u>Correct Translation</u>
Eternal life	Zoë Aionios	The life of the ages
Life eternal	Zoë Aionios	The life of the ages
Everlasting life	Zoë Aionios	The life of the ages
Life everlasting	Zoë Aionios	The life of the ages

Jesus is Zoë. He said in John 14:6 "I am the way, the

truth, and the life (Zoë): no man cometh unto the Father, but by me." The infinite life that Jesus is, is now manifested in time and space, or, into the Ages. Ephesians 2:7 declares: That in the ages to come he might shew the exceeding riches of his grace in his kindness toward us through Jesus Christ.

John 3:16

Even the most beloved Bible verse in the world has been mistranslated in most Bibles, which in the aftermath, has led to more misunderstanding:

For God so loved the world, that he gave his only begotten Son, that whosoever believeth in him should not perish, but have everlasting life (Zoe Aionios).

The Greek word for "in", is - eis, which means – "into" - Ephesians 4:15 says: "But speaking the truth in love, may grow up into (eis) him in all things, which is the head, even Christ." We believe "into" Jesus, as we are progressively saved, Spirit, Soul, and Body, which is explained in subsequent sections of this book. The word – perish, does not mean -go into eternal damnation. This is not what is says. The Greek word is – apollumi, it is used in Mark 4:38, when the disciples were concerned about dying in the storm on the sea and said, "Master, carest thou not that we <u>perish</u> (apollumi)?" They did not say, "Carest thou that we go to eternal damnation?"

With these thoughts in mind, here is how John 3:16 should be translated:

For God so loved the world, that he gave his only begotten Son, that whosoever believeth into him should not die, but have the life of the ages.

Jesus said to Martha in John 11:26 - And whosoever liveth and believeth in (eis = into) me shall never die? Believeth thou this?

The Wages of Sin is Death

Romans 6:23 states, "For the wages of sin is death; but the gift of God is eternal life (Greek: The life of the ages) through Jesus Christ our Lord." When some people hear this verse they assume death means - eternal damnation. If that is true, to be consistent, we need to change the word – death, in the Bible, to - eternal damnation. Here is how some of the verses would sound:

Genesis 25:11 And it came to pass after the *eternal damnation* of Abraham, that God blessed his son Issac.

Genesis 27:10 (Rebekah speaking to Jacob concerning Isaac) And thou shalt bring it the thy father, that he may eat, and that he may bless thee before his *eternal damnation.*

Psalm 23:4 Yea, though I walk through the valley of the shadow of *eternal damnation*, I will fear no evil.

Romans 5:12 By one man sin entered into the world, and *eternal damnation* by sin; so *eternal damnation* passed upon all men.

Philippians 2:8 He humbled himself, and became obedient unto *eternal damnation*, even the *eternal damnation* of the cross.

Revelation 20:14 And *eternal damnation* and hell were cast into the lake of fire. This is the second *eternal damnation.*

Again, as stated in Chapter Three, if the wages of sin was eternal damnation, Jesus never paid the price for our sin.

The Unpardonable Sin?

Another passage of scripture where the truth is indecipherable, unless you uncover the Greek words, is Matthew 12:31-32: Wherefore I say unto you, All manner of sin and blasphemy shall be forgiven unto men: but the blasphemy against the Holy Ghost shall not be forgiven unto men. And whosoever speaketh a word against the Son of man, it shall be forgiven him: but whosoever speaketh against the Holy Ghost, it shall not be forgiven him, neither in this world, neither in the world to come.

The key to strip away the illusion of the <u>Unpardonable Sin,</u> lies in the last line of verse 32: "Neither in the world (Aion = Age) neither in the world (Age) to come." The Interlinear reads: "Neither in this age, nor the coming one." Jesus spoke this verse while in the Age of Law. The following age would be the Church Age. However, there is an Age called the Age of Ages, or, the Dispensation of the Fullness of Times, when all things in heaven and earth will be gathered into Christ (Ephesians 1:10).

According to John 16:8-9, Sin is unbelief, - "And when he (The Holy Spirit) is come, he will reprove the world of sin, and of righteousness, and of judgment: <u>of sin, because they believe not on me.</u>" Hence, if we are in unbelief, we are not forgiven. However, Romans 3:3-4 declares: "For what if some did not believe: shall their unbelief make the faith of God without effect? GOD FORBID: yea, let God be true, but every man a liar; as it is written, That thou mightest be justified in thy sayings, and mightest overcome when thou are judged."

Consequently, the Unpardonable Sin is just one more fabrication of the religions of mortal men. All of the Judgments of God are corrective in nature. Hence, words like damned, damnation, condemned, and condemnation, if searched in the Greek, will validate the corrective process of God in bringing us unto Him.

Endless

Hebrews 7:16 speaking of Jesus being after the Order of Melchizedek states: Who is made, not after the carnal commandment, but after the power of an endless life.

The word – endless, is the Greek word – Akatalutos, which means, eternal, as permanent. Since this Greek word does mean eternal or endless, why was the word *Endless* not translated onto other Greek words in the Book of Hebrews, as well as the rest of the New Testament where the word Aionios was used?. It is because all the derivations of Aion, such as Aionios and Aionion do not mean endless, as eternal.

For Ever and Ever

Just as there is a servant of servants (Genesis 9:25), the God of gods (Deuteronomy 10:17), The Song of songs (SOS 1:1), the Vanity of vanities (Ecclesiastes 12:8), a Prince of princes (Daniel 8:25), a Hebrew of Hebrews

(Philippians 3:5), the King of kings and Lord of lords (I Timothy 6:15), so also there is the - Age of Ages:

Hebrews 1:8 declares, "But unto the Son, he saith, Thy throne O God, is for <u>ever and</u> <u>ever</u>: a scepter of righteousness is the scepter of thy kingdom."

Ever and ever, in the Greek Interlinear Bible reveals the Age of the Ages (aiona of the aionos). This same principle is found in other Scriptures that use the phrase *for ever and ever*. For instance, Ephesians 3:21: Unto him be glory in the church by Jesus Christ throughout all ages, world without end. Amen.

The word - world, in the Greek means Ages. This reveals the continuum of the glory of God on Earth. Ephesians 3:21 in Young's Literal Translation says - To him is the glory in the assembly in Christ Jesus, to all the generations of the age of the ages (aionos of the aionion). Amen.

There are also passages that use the phrase - for ever and ever, when speaking of the judgment of those with the mark of the beast (Revelation 14:11), Babylon (Revelation 19:3), and of the beast and false prophet (Revelation 20:10). Once you have read Chapter Five - The Trichotomy, you will understand what the Beast is, and realize that his judgment is not for eternity, he is simply evaporated. Hence - For ever and ever, or the Age of the Ages, is simply showing the completeness of an event.

Matthew 12:20 states: A bruised reed shall he not break, and a smoking flax shall he not quench, till he send forth judgment unto victory.

What saith the Scholars

The following is a list of respected Bible scholars who agree that the Greek word – Aionios, along with it's derivations, have nothing to do with our understanding of the word - Eternal, but they make reference to the Ages.

1. Professor Martin Vincent: Word Studies of the New Testament, Volume 4 pages 58-62.
2. Professor William Barclay: Barclays Autobiography (Letters of the Corinthians).
3. Dr. R.F. Weymouth: New Testament in Modern Speech, page 657
4. C.J. Ellicott: Commentary on the whole Bible.
5. Professor A.B. Bruce: Expositors Greek New Testament.
6. W.E. Vine: Vine's Expository Dictionary of New Testament Words
7. J.B. Lightfoot: Commentary on the Epistles of St. Paul
8. Professor Robert Young: Young's Analytical Concordance
9. Dr. Nigel Turner: Christian Words, page 457.
10. Dr. R.F. Farrar: The Life of Christ and The Life and Work of St. Paul.

Listed below are some Bibles that have correctly translated Aion and its derivations:

1. Young's Literal Translation
2. Rotherhams Emphasized Bible
3. Emphatic Diaglott
4. American Standard Version (periodically)
5. Concordant Version
6. New Testament in Modern Speech (Weymouth)

7. King James Version Companion Bible (by E.W. Bullinger)

Other Bible Study manuals that are resourceful on this topic are:

1. Liddell and Scott's Greek-English Lexicon
2. Thesaurus Dictionary of the English Language
3. Shedd Theological Dictionary
4. Earnest Weekly's Etymological Dictionary of Modern English
5. Thayer's Greek-English Lexicon
6. Encyclopedic Dictionary of the Bible
7. The Interpreters Dictionary of the Bible; Volume 4, page 643
8. Triglot Dictionary of Representative Words in Hebrew, Greek and English
9. The Pulpit Commentary:; Volume 15, page 485
10. The Parkhurst Lexicon
11. Lange's Commentary American Edition; Volume 5, page 48

Louis Abbott

In my research on this topic, I was fortunate to eventually run into the writings of Louis Abbott. I found his research to be refreshingly thorough. Not one of my questions went unanswered to my initially skeptical mind. Louis was a pastor of a small church who was challenged one day on his belief in Eternal Damnation. He took up the challenge, after three years of intensive research of the Greek and Hebrew words behind the English words hell, eternal punishment, and everlasting destruction, Louis quit his job as a pastor and continued his studies. He took Greek courses at Moody Bible Institute, Loyola University and other schools. His personal library consists of thousands of Bible reference books and probably more books on New Testament Greek than most Bible Colleges and Seminaries.

For almost 50 years, Louis has been studying the subject matter included in this chapter. If I have not touched upon a certain scripture that you are thinking of, we are fortunate now through the Internet to expedite our own research. You may find the answer to your question in Mr. Abbott's <u>Analytical Study of Words,</u> through the Google search engine.

Vital Signs
Album: Moving Pictures

Unstable condition:
A symptom of life
In mental,
And environmental
Change

Atmospheric disturbance –
The feverish flux,
O human interface
And interchange
The impulse is pure -
Sometimes our circuits get shorted,
By external interference

Signals get crossed –
And the balance distorted
By internal incoherence

A tired mind become a shape-shifter
Everybody need a mood lifter
Everybody need reverse polarity

Everybody got mixed feelings
About the function and the form
Everybody got to deviate
From the norm

An ounce of perception –
A pound of obscure,
Process information
At half speed

Pause:
Rewind – replay –
Warm memory chip
Random – sample –
Hold the one you need

Leave out the fiction –
The fact is;
This friction,
Can only be worn by persistence

Leave out conditions –
Courageous convictions,
Will drag the dream into existence

A tired mind become a shape-shifter
Everybody need a soft filter
Everybody need reverse polarity
Everybody got mixed feelings
About the function and the form
Everybody got to elevate
From the norm

CHAPTER FIVE

The Trichotomy

I will praise thee; for I am fearfully and wonderfully made:
marvelous are thy works; and that my soul
knoweth right well.
- Psalm 139:14

Commercials and magazine ads are created for us to fly on their magic carpet with sentimental ease. The corporate world endeavors to ingratiate themselves into the needs of the body and soul – they do this by making an effort to create urgency in your mind through desire or fear. Every marketing department has a quota – they need to convince us that their latest product will vibrantly refresh or invigorate us:

Mind, body, and soul - or
Body, mind, and spirit - or
Soul, body, and mind -
Etcetera...

Which one is it? This concentration has been the exact opposite of God - the perfection of imperfection. The true order of who we are has been inscripted in I Thessalonians 5:23:

> "And the very God of peace sanctify you wholly; and I pray God your whole spirit and soul and body be preserved blameless unto the coming of our Lord Jesus Christ."

You are a Spirit.
You have a Soul (mind, will, and emotions).
You live in a Body.

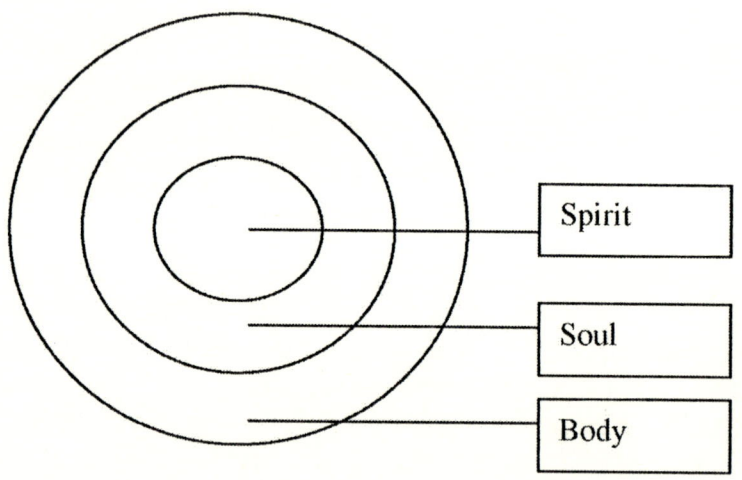

A rudimentary parallel of the function of Spirit, Soul, and Body, can be clarified through the analogy of a movie projector and the screen:

The Spirit is the light of the projector.
The Soul, as the projector - contains the slide or film being

played.

Whatever habitual image is in your mind (your tapes), is projected by the Spirit, through your Soul and into your Body or external world – the screen.

Proverbs 23:7 states: As a man thinketh in his heart, so is he.

The Spirit

When a person is spiritually reborn, their spirit (who they really are), is illuminated as the presence of Jesus, the Light of Life, comes into their heart - as the Holy Spirit. Their spirit immediately become one with God. This sacred event can be likened to a light bulb being turned on. Jesus said in Matthew 6:23 "If the light that is in you is darkness, how great is that darkness." The following scriptures clarify the *spiritual dynamic* of the trinity that we are in the image of God:

Psalm 51:10 The Lord shall put a new and right spirit within me.

Ezekiel 11:19 And I will give them one heart, and I will put a new spirit within you.

Zechariah 12:1 God forms the spirit of man within him.

Malachi 2:15 Take heed to your spirit.

Luke 1:17 My spirit rejoices in God my Savior.

Romans 1:9 I serve God with my spirit.

Romans 8:16 It is the Spirit himself that bears witness with our spirit that we are children of God.

I Corinthians 6:17 He that is joined to the Lord is one spirit with him.

The Soul

The Soul consists of our mind, will, and emotions:

With our mind we can see a mountain.
With our will we may choose to go skiing.
With our emotions we can feel the adrenaline-rush through the body.

The next stage after our spirit has been renewed, is the regeneration of our soul. This happens as we spend time in communion with the Father of Lights and begin to bring our mind, will, and emotions into progressive conformity to the timeless truth of the Word of God. The Bible calls this being conformed to the image of God - the heavenly image (Romans 8:29 and I Corinthians 15:49). The following passages show the distinction of the spirit and soul:

Luke 1:46-47 And Mary said, My soul doth magnify the Lord, and my spirit hath rejoiced in God my Saviour.

I Corinthians 15:45 And so it is written, The first man Adam was made a living soul; the last Adam was made a quickening spirit.

Hebrew 4:12 For the word of God is quick and powerful, and sharper than any two-edged sword, piercing even to the dividing asunder of soul and spirit, and of the joints and marrow, and is a discerner of the thoughts and intents of the heart.

Hebrews 10:39 But we are not of them who draw back unto perdition; but of them that believe to the saving of the soul.

I Peter 1:9 Receiving the end of your faith, even the salvation of your souls.

I Peter 1:22-23 Seeing ye have purified your souls in obeying the truth through the Spirit unto unfeigned love of the brethren, see that ye love one another with a pure heart fervently: Being born again, not of corruptible seed, but of incorruptible, by the word of God, which liveth and abideth for ever.

If we are not being conformed to the image of Jesus, we will spend most of our time living in the soulish realm, being conformed to the image of the beast (Revelation 15:2). This is the realm of darkness, fear, and confusion. If we live in the soul - rather than the spirit, we will be standing in our own way from receiving the power, faith, and light of the Holy Spirit within.

The Body

The third and final realm of who we are, that is in obvious need of salvation, is the body. The Apostle Paul wrote in Romans 7:24 "O wretched man that I am! Who shall deliver me from this body of death?" The answer is - Jesus will. I Corinthians 15:26 says: The last enemy that shall be destroyed is death.

When Adam and Eve fell, their fall was from out of the immortal presence of God, into the mundane realm of being mortal. Jesus Christ is the way back into immortality. Jesus is the way, the truth, and the life (John 14:6). To say that immortality is impossible is to place a limit on our spiritual growth, and place a limit on God, with whom all things are possible (Matthew 19:26).

This issue will be addressed in Chapter Eleven— Imagining Immortality.

The Enemy Within

When Jesus was alone in the Judean wilderness, fasting under the scorching heat of the desert sun, for forty days and forty nights, while being tempted of the devil (Matthew 4:1-11), He was not dealing with some freak-entity on the outside of Himself - rather, He was being tempted by his earthly nature. I Corinthians 15: 45 says: Jesus was the Last Adam. The following passage, (and the rest of this chapter) reveals that the Devil is nothing more than a Biblical personification of Adam, The Old Man (Colossians 3:9).

> Hebrews 2:14 states: Forasmuch then as the children are partakers of flesh and blood, he also himself likewise took part of the same; that through death he might destroy him that had the power of death, that is, the devil. (CF: Ephesians 2:15-16).

Jesus was tempted with His earthly nature just as we are. If you have ever embarked on a period of fasting, you know how strong the voice of the flesh can be. That Old Man in you is doing the push-pump-and–pull, screaming to go down to Wendy's for a Triple Stack with large fries, washed down with a large Frosty. After that, the Devil might even try talking you into heading down to the bakery for some key lime pie.

Many times in the Bible, Jesus is referred to as the Son of Man, denoting that He was as much of a human being as you and I. Personally, in my times of temptation, I have never been approached by someone in the external realm that I would consider the Devil. However, it is uncanny that on every occasion that I decide to fast, people start offering me free food. They are not the Devil, but the Devil = The Old Man, - in me, is always telling me to – "go ahead and eat, you can always start fasting tomorrow." The following passages highlight that Jesus was tempted as we are, yet without sin:

Romans 8:3 God sent his own Son in the likeness of sinful flesh, and for sin, condemned sin in the flesh.

Phil 2:7 Christ was made in the likeness of men.

Hebrews 4:15 Jesus was in all points tempted like as we are yet without sin.

Hebrews 9:14 Christ who through the eternal spirit offered himself without spot to God.

I Peter 1:18-19 We are redeemed with the precious blood of Christ, as of a lamb without blemish and without spot.

I Peter 2:22 Christ did no sin, neither was guile found in his mouth.

I John 3:5 He was manifested to take away our sins; and in him is no sin.

Lucifer

In Isaiah 14:12-17 and Ezekiel 28:11-19, we have the account of the fall of Lucifer, son of the morning, the anointed cherub. I grew up with the teaching that Lucifer was this beautiful angel in heaven commissioned to lead the heavenly choirs in their celestial anthems unto God. Then suddenly one day - Lucifer became inflated with pride because he was so beautiful and decided he wanted to rule the universe, so he attempted to overthrow the Throne. Luckily, God won the fray and threw Lucifer down to earth where he became the Devil.

Scoping in on Isaiah 14:16 "They that see thee shall narrowly look upon thee, and consider thee saying, Is this the man that made the earth to tremble, that did shake kingdoms." This man is Adam - that brought sin and death into the earth. Romans 5:12 states: "By one man sin entered the world." Adam was the son of the morning by virtue of being a son of God (Luke 3:38). Jesus, the creator of Adam, is the Bright and Morning Star (Revelation 22:16).

So then, Lucifer = The Old Man = The First Man Adam, within us - is still trying to exalt himself above God = The New Man = Jesus = The Second Man.

The Serpent in the Garden

That Old Serpent, is the Devil, and Satan.
(Revelation 12:9 and Revelation 20:2)

When Adam and Eve were tempted of the serpent in the Garden of Eden, were they tempted by a literal talking snake? Or, is there something more elaborate going on here to illustrate the sinful and fallen nature of the First Man, Adam? (Genesis 5:2 And he called their name Adam).

Genesis 2:7 And the Lord God formed man of the dust of the ground, and breathed into his nostrils the breath of life; and man became a living soul. (Nephesh).

Genesis 2:19 Out of the ground the Lord God formed every beast of the field, and every fowl of the air; and brought them unto Adam to see what he would call them: and whatsoever Adam called every living creature (Nephesh), that was the name thereof.

Genesis 3:1 Now the serpent was more subtil than any beast of the field which the Lord God had made.

The serpent, who is the Devil and Satan, was formed from the dust of the ground, not formed as an angel in heaven.

The Spiritual Interpretation of the Serpent

The serpent was formed from the dust of the ground. He is included in every beast of the field. Since the serpent is the Devil, the traditional view that he came from heaven is immediately blown out of the water. If the Devil was an actual talking snake, where is this suspicious-looking stranger today? Where are his offspring?

These questions are why Western religion has attempted to throw sands in our eyes by telling us that - Satan came in the form of a serpent. However, the Bible does not say that – it clearly states: That old serpent is the Devil and Satan. God told the serpent in Genesis 3:14 "Upon thy belly shalt thou go, and dust shalt thou eat all the days of thy life." Has anyone seen where this snake called Satan has been crawling around lately?

The literal interpretation is ridiculous.

The spiritual interpretation is that the serpent, who is the Devil and Satan - is the serpentine nature of The First Man, Adam = The Old Man (Ephesians 4:22). The Devil is simply a spiritual personification of the Adamic nature of our soul that has yet to be conformed into the image of Christ (Romans 8:29). Rather, it is conformed to the image of the beast (Revelation 15:2). Our mortal self, which feeds off the dust of the earthly nature, is that Old Serpent. The serpent that was more subtil than any beast of the field (Genesis 3:1).

Psalm 44:25 For our soul is bowed down to the dust: our belly cleaveth unto the earth.

Isaiah 29:4 (Of the city of Ariel) And thou shalt be brought down, and shalt speak out of the ground, and thy speech shall be low out of the dust, and thy voice shall be, as of one that hath a familiar spirit, out of the ground, and thy speech shall whisper out of the dust.

Micah 7:17 (Of wicked nations) They shall lick the dust like a serpent, they shall move out of their holes like worms of the earth.

Satan means Adversary

In the Bible, the Devil is always a Satan, however, a Satan is not always the Devil.

Technically, the word – Satan, in the Hebrew language, means, Adversary. Hence, in complete harmony with the true Biblical meaning of Satan - The visiting team in a football game is Satan to the home team.

In Numbers 22:22 and 32, we see that the Angel of the Lord was an adversary against Balaam - the prophet for profit. The Hebrew word for adversary, is Satan. Here again, another account of translational bias, in not understanding what the word of God was intending:

Verse 22: And God's anger was kindled because he went: and the angel of the Lord stood in the way for an adversary (Satan) against him. Now he was riding on his ass, and his two servants were with him.

Verse 32: And the angel of the Lord said unto him, Wherefore hast thou smitten thine ass these three times? Behold, I went out to <u>withstand</u> (Hebrew word is Satan) thee, because thy way is perverse before me.

Provided below are some other Biblical accounts where adversaries were called Satan in Hebrew text:

I Samuel 29:4 (paraphrased) And the princes of the Philistines were wroth with David, he and said, He is an adversary (Satan) unto us.

II Samuel 19:22 And David said, What have I to do with you, ye sons of Zeruiah, that ye should this day be adversaries (Satan) unto me?

Other scriptures you may want to look up that reveal the same are: I Kings 5:4; I Kings 11:14,23, 25; Psalm 38:20; 71:13; 109:4,20,29.

Note: I'm not yet finished with my teaching of Satan in the Book of Job. I do plan on providing it in future editions of this book.

When Jesus called Peter Satan

Matthew 16:21-23 From that time forth began Jesus to shew unto his disciples, how that he must go unto Jerusalem, and suffer many things of the elders and chief priests and scribes, and be killed, and be raised again the third day. Then Peter took him, and began to rebuke him saying: Be it far from thee, Lord: this shall not be unto thee. But <u>he turned, and said unto Peter, Get thee behind me, Satan</u>: thou art an offence unto me: for thou savourest not the things that be of God, but those that be of men.

It does not say that, Jesus said unto Satan - in Peter, behind Peter, above Peter, or under Peter. It clearly states that Jesus called Peter - Satan. Why? In this instance, Peter was operating out of his Soul = his earthly nature = The First Man Adam = The Old Man. Moments before, Peter was operating from his Spirit = his heavenly nature = The New Man, when Jesus said to him: Blessed art thou Simon Barjona: for flesh and blood hath not revealed it unto thee, but my Father which is in heaven (Matthew 16:17).

John 8:44

Jesus also rebukes the Scribes and Pharisees after they boast of being Abraham's seed. Jesus admits that they are of the natural linage of Abraham, yet, because the word of God had no place in them, he says: "Ye are of your father the devil, and the lusts of your father ye will do. He was a murderer from the beginning, and abode not in the truth, because there is no truth in him." The religious systems tell us the Devil was a beautiful Angel from the beginning – however, the Alpha and Omega said he was a murderer from the beginning.

Genesis 1:11 says: "Every seed is in itself." Jesus calls the Scribes and Pharisees the children = the offspring= the seed, of the Devil, because they were not doing the works of Abraham – which is living by faith (Romans 4:13-21).

Two Seeds

Genesis 3:14-15 And the Lord said unto the serpent, Because thou hast done this, thou art cursed above all cattle, and above every beast of the field; upon thy belly shalt thou go, and dust shalt thou eat all the days of thy life: <u>And I will put enmity between thee and the women, and between thy seed and her seed;</u> it shall bruise thy head, and thou shalt bruise his heel.

I Corinthians 15:45-48 And so it is written, The first man Adam was made a living soul; the last Adam was made a quickening spirit. Howbeit that was not first which is spiritual, but that which is natural; and afterward that which is spiritual. The first man is of the earth, earthy: the second man is the Lord from heaven. As is the earthy, such are they also that are earthy: and as is the heavenly, such are they also that are heavenly.

According to the two scriptures above, there are only two seeds in the earth. From these two seemingly simple passages, we can conclude the following:

1. The Seed of the Serpent = The First Man Adam =

The Old Man = The Soul (unregenerated) =The Anti-Christ = The Devil.

2. The Seed of Eve = The Last Adam = The Second Man = The New Man = The Spirit = Christ = The Lord from Heaven.

The Anti-Christ

Every time we look in the mirror, and know that we have spent more time that day sowing to the flesh than sowing to the spirit, we are seeing the reflection of the Anti-Christ. We see prophets of wind (Jeremiah 5:13) on television and have read books - that someday there will be a man that shall rise up and take the nations by storm, making his throne in modern day Jerusalem. Nothing could be farther from the truth, those that attempt to teach on the Anti-Christ, almost invariably never open to the five places in the New Testament where Anti-Christ is mentioned:

1. and 2. I John 2:18 Little children, it is the last time: and as you have heard Anti-Christ shall come, and even now there are many Anti-Christ's; whereby we know that it is the last time.

3. I John 2:22 Who is a liar but he that denieth that Jesus is the Christ. He is Anti-Christ, that denieth the Father and the Son.

4. I John 4:3 Every spirit that confesseth not that Jesus Christ is come in the flesh is not of God: and this is the spirit of Anti-Christ whereof ye have heard that it should come; and even now already it is in the world.

5. II John 7 For many deceivers are entered into the world who confess not that Jesus Christ is come in the flesh.

Strange, the Word of God says the Anti-Christ existed in the first century and even now. Seems to me that those looking for the Anti-Christ to set up shop in Jerusalem may be preaching a false doctrine. Every time we deny the word of God, we deny Jesus. This is being Anti-Christ.

Taking it to the next level, in I John 4:3 and II John 7, the Greek word for – come, is Erchomai, which is a present tense verb. It should be translated to - coming. Jesus is coming in the flesh, not His flesh that he walked in 2000 years ago. He is coming within us, the Body of Christ, that this mortal shall put on immortality. Those that teach otherwise, are the Anti-Christ. No doubt, there are many Anti-Christ's out there.

The Man of Sin

II Thessalonians 2:3-8 is a key passage that is misconstrued to support the idea of the foreboding reign of some person in the Middle East called the Anti-Christ. As we examine these scriptures in the spiritual present tense, its laughable how this belief could gain such popularity. The reason is - high drama sells.

Verse 3: Let no man deceive you by any means: for that day shall not come, except there come a falling away first, and that man of sin be revealed, the son of perdition.

There must be a falling away of any concept that we have had of any Anti-Christ outside of ourselves. When the mortal nature within us is finally identified as the man of sin = The Old Man = The First Adam, then we are free to begin understanding the ascension of the New Man = Christ, within us.

Verse 4: Who opposeth and exalteth himself above all that is called God, or that is worshipped; so that he as God sitteth in the temple of God, shewing himself that he is God.

If we interpret the Bible with the Bible, it is clear that the Body of Christ is the temple of God:

I Corinthians 3:16 Know ye not that ye are the temple of God, and that the Spirit of God dwelleth in you.

I Corinthians 6:19 What? Know ye not that your body is the temple of the Holy Ghost which is in you, which ye have of God, and ye are not your own.

II Corinthians 6:16 And what agreement hath the temple of God with idols? For ye are the temple of the living God; as God hath said, I will dwell in them, and walk in them; and I will be their God, and they shall be my people.

Ephesians 2:19-21 Now therefore ye are no more strangers and foreigners, but fellowcitizens with the saints, and of the household of God; And are built upon the foundation of the apostles and prophets, Jesus Christ himself being the chief corner stone; In whom all the building fitly framed together groweth unto an holy temple in the Lord.

Hebrews 3:6 But Christ as a son over his own house; whose house are we, if we hold fast the confidence and the rejoicing of the hope firm unto the end.

Every time the carnal soulish realm = The Old Man, within us, denies the promptings of the Holy Spirit and the Word of God = Jesus Christ, he is exalting himself above God. Anyone that is being Anti-The Word of God , is automatically being Anti-Christ. Revelation 19:13 says, the name of Jesus is - The Word of God.

Verse 5: Remember ye not, that when I was yet with you, I told you these things?

When the letters of Paul circulated among the churches, he expected them to understand that they were the temple of God.

Verse 6: And now ye know what he withholdeth that he might be revealed in his time.

He that withholdeth the ascension of the New Man within us, is the Old Man = The son of perdition. We must choose to fast, pray, and meditate the word of God, to grow spiritually. If not, the Old Man is still withholding you from receiving all the joy, peace, and blessing that Jesus has in store for you.

Verse 7: For the mystery of iniquity doth already work: only he who now letteth will let, until he be taken out of the way.

In Romans 7:15-17 The Apostle Paul states – " For that which I do I allow not: for what I would, that do I not; but what I hate, that I do." He goes on to say – "Now then, it is no more I that do it, but sin that dwelleth in me" - this is the mystery of iniquity. The mystery of iniquity is very apparent when someone in authority tells us to do something that is against the grain of our independent nature. Many times our first instinct is to do the opposite.

Verse 8: And then shall that Wicked be revealed, whom the Lord shall consume with the spirit of his mouth, and shall destroy with the brightness of his coming.

As our imagination is renewed to the word of God, which is the spirit of his mouth, our soulish man comes into conformity with the Lord. As the presence of Jesus, the Bright and Morning Star increases in us, the Old Man is evaporated.

Spiritual Wickedness in High Places

Ephesians 6:11-13 Put on the whole armour of God, (Ephesians 6:14-18) that ye may be able to stand against the wiles of the devil. For we wrestle not against flesh and blood, but against principalities, against powers, against rulers of the darkness of this world, against spiritual wickedness in high places.

The wiles of the devil are known in this passage as: principalities, powers, rules of darkness and spiritual wickedness in high places. The ultimate intention of this book is to help everyone understand that the will of God for us is to be made whole - Spirit, Soul, and Body, to overflow with the presence of God, living in the fullness of His joy. Yet, there is a war going on here. It is a war between our Spirit and our Flesh. The battleground is the Soul (mind, will, and emotions). With this in mind, the following scriptures will be provided (interpreting the Bible with the Bible) to clarify that the wiles of the devil, is the spiritual wickedness that wars within us.

> Romans 7:23 But I see another law in my members, warring against the law of my mind, and bring me into captivity to the law of sin which is in my members.

> II Corinthians 10:3-6 For though we walk in the flesh, we do not war after the flesh: For the weapons or our warfare are not carnal, but mighty through God to the pulling down of strong holds; Casting down imaginations, and every high thing that exalteth itself against the knowledge of God, and bringing into captivity every thought to the obedience of Christ; And having in a readiness to revenge all disobedience, when your obedience is fulfilled.

These strongholds and high things that exalt themselves against the Word of God - exist in our thoughts, our will, our emotions, and the imaginations of our Soul. They are without question principalities, powers, rulers of the darkness, and spiritual wickedness in high places, which war within us against the working of the Word and the Spirit.

Evil Spirits

In the past, I believed evil spirits and demons were invisible little gremlins jetting through the spirit world waiting to possess us to control us as in the movie *The Exorcist*. From there, I reasoned from Hebrews 12:23 which mentions "spirits of just men made perfect" that, this must presuppose *spirits of unjust men not made perfect*, which must be the evil spirits spoken of in the Bible.

There was one problem with both of these views, Jesus said in Mark 7:23 "All these evil things come from within, and defile a man." I now believe, if we continue to live in the nature of Adam = The Old Man, we will have all kinds of evil spirits: spirits of lust, spirits of greed, seducing spirits, spirits of error, spirit of bitterness, etc. If we nurture this evil spirit within us, it can grow into a raging demon. The following verses attest to this:

> Ephesians 2:1-3 And you hath he quickened, who were dead in trespasses and sins; Wherein in time past ye walked according to the course of this world, according to the prince of the power of the air, <u>the spirit that now worketh in the children of disobedience</u>: Among whom also we all had our conversation in times past in the lusts of the flesh, fulfilling the desires of the flesh and of the mind; and were by nature the children of wrath, even as others.

Some people ask: Can a Christian have a devil? My answer is: If they want to.

> Ephesians 4:23-23 That ye put off concerning the former conversation, the old man, which is corrupt in according to the deceitful lusts; And be renewed in the spirit of your mind.

If we are not renewed in the spirit of our mind, the spirit of our mind is spiritual wickedness. Which leads to all kinds of unrighteousness and evil, spirits.

> James 4:5 Do you think that the scripture saith in vain, The spirit that dwelleth in us lusteth to envy?

Closer To The Heart
Album: A Farewell To Kings

And the men who hold high places
Must be the ones who start
To mould a new reality
Closer to the Heart
The Blacksmith and the Artist
Reflect it in their art
Forge their creativity
Closer to the Heart
Philosophers and Ploughmen
Each must know his part
To sow a new mentality
Closer to the Heart
You can be the Captain
I will draw the Chart
Sailing into destiny
Closer to the Heart

CHAPTER SIX

The Doctrine of the Alpha and Omega

We struggle with complexities, and avoid the simplicities.
- Norman Vincent Peale

The place to begin teaching true Biblical Doctrine begins in Hebrews 6:1-2 – The Doctrine of Christ. This section of the book is vitally important - through understanding the Doctrine of Christ, we clearly understand the will of God for our spiritual journey. It is through the Doctrine of Christ that we all come unto the unity of the faith and of the knowledge of the Son of God unto a perfect man (Ephesians 4:13). The Doctrine of Christ is the full counsel of God (Acts 20:27).

Second Timothy 4:3-4 declares: "The time will come when people will not endure sound doctrine; but after there own lusts will heap upon themselves teachers, having itching ears; And they shall turn away their ears from the truth, and shall be turned unto fables." This is a fulfillment of Amos 8:11-13 where the Lord says: "He shall send a famine of the <u>hearing of the word of the Lord</u>. Where the people shall wander from sea to sea, from north to south (or, from church to church and convention to convention) to seek the word of the Lord, and shall not find it. And the fair virgins and young men shall faint for thirst."

My doctrine is not mine, but his that sent me. If any man will do his will, he shall know of the doctrine, whether it be of God, or whether I speak of myself (John 7:16-17).

Whosoever transgresseth, and abideth not in the doctrine of Christ, hath not God. He that abideth in the doctrine of Christ, he hath both the Father and the Son. If there come any unto you and bring not this doctrine, receive him not into your house, neither bid him God speed: For he that biddeth him God speed is partaker of his evil deeds (II John 9-11).

Question: What is Sound Doctrine?
Answer: Sound Doctrine is the Doctrine of Christ in Hebrews 6:1-2.

Ephesians 2:20 We are built upon the foundation of apostles and prophets, Jesus Christ himself being the chief cornerstone.

Acts 2:42 The disciples continued steadfastly in the Apostles Doctrine.

Hence, the foundation of our doctrine should be built around Christ - The Doctrine of Christ.

The Doctrine of Christ

Hebrews 6:1-3 states: Therefore leaving the principles of the doctrine of Christ, let us go unto perfection; not laying again the foundation of

Repentance from Dead Works
Faith Toward God,
The Doctrine of Baptisms
The Laying On Of Hands
The Resurrection From The Dead
Eternal Judgment (The Greek reads: The Judgment of the Ages)

And this we will do, if God permit.

The Milk and the Meat

The preceding list are the six elements in the foundation of The Doctrine of Christ = The Apostles Doctrine = Sound Doctrine. In Hebrews 5:12 they are referred to as, "The first principles of the oracles of God" - The Milk. It says, "Not laying again." However, if the church you go to, conventions you attend, books you read, tapes you listen to, videos and DVD's and ministries you watch, have not, or, are not teaching and preaching, and prophesying, the Doctrine of Christ, how can you lay it again? Believe me, God is definitely permitting us to declare the Doctrine of Christ.

The Meat of the Word of God is – Going onto Perfection. I get a kick out of preachers who tout Malachi 3:10 "Bring ye all the tithes into the storehouse, that there may be meat in mine house." Why would we want to throw our money away to churches that not only do not preach the meat of – Going onto Perfection, but are uncomfortable ve

when the milk becomes a little warm?

Some might say: "Anyone can open the Bible and start reading or teaching from it." This is true, however, without any hesitation. Hebrews 6:1-2 is where we are to begin laying the foundation of our spiritual belief system - if we want to obey the Lord Jesus Christ.

To deny the word of God is to deny Jesus Christ. Our call is to – Go onto Perfection. However, we will not understand the ultimate intention of God, if the Doctrine of Christ is not established as the foundation in our life. We can't lay again what has not yet been established.

It is the will of God that every believer should have the eyes of their understanding enlightened in the Doctrine of Christ – otherwise, we will be constantly driven from uncertainty to uncertainty, carried here and there by every wind of doctrine. This is certainly true today – ask your local apostle, prophet, evangelist, pastor, teacher, priest, bishop, or minister - What is the Doctrine of Christ? If they state anything other than Hebrews 6:1-2, they are askew. If they do not come in line with the Word of God and start preaching the Truth, you should take heed to II John 9-11 and leave that church - without letting the door hit you in the back. Then meditate on the scriptures provided in Chapter Nine – Meeting Jesus Outside The Box.

The following is a short synopsis of each spiritual principle in the foundation of the Doctrine of Christ:

Repentance from Dead Works

When we enter our relationship with Jesus, it is absolutely imperative to know that there is nothing we can do to be accepted and loved by Him. We are not accepted by Him through going to church, feeding the hungry, being a minister, or any other Dead Works. The subsequent scriptures attest to this truth:

Matthew 7:22-23 Many will say to me in that day, Lord, Lord, have we not prophesied in thy name? and in thy name have cast out devils? and in thy name done many wonderful works? And then I will profess unto them, I never knew you: depart from me, ye that work iniquity.

Galatians 5:4 Christ is become of no effect unto you, whosoever of you are justified by the law; ye are fallen from grace.

Faith Toward God

As we make the 180 degree turn from Dead Works, we then move into - Faith Toward God:

Ephesians 2:8-9 For by grace are ye saved through faith; and that not of yourselves: it is the gift of God: Not of works, lest any man should boast.

Hebrews 11:6 But without faith it is impossible to please God: for he that cometh to God must believe that he is, and that he is a rewarder of them that diligently seek him.

Faith in God is different from Belief in God. We can believe there is a God, but not have faith that He will bless us. For instance, if a friend of yours that you trust, promised you that she or he was going to buy you a new car, would you thank your friend before or after you had the car? If you really trusted their word, you would thank them before you

119

received the car. Likewise, there are many promises in the Bible stating that the Lord will bless you. All you need to do is have faith in His word. The essence of what Faith is can be discovered in the following two passages:

Mark 11:22-24 And Jesus answered saying to them, Have faith in God. Truly I say to you, whoever says to this mountain, Be taken up and cast into the sea, and does not doubt in his heart, but believes that what he says is going to happen, it shall be granted to him. Therefore I say to you, all things for which you pray and ask, underline believe that you have received them, and they shall be granted to you. (New American Standard Version)

Hebrews 11:1 Now faith is the substance of things hoped for, the evidence of things not seen.

Faith is like a muscle - the more you renew your heart and mind to the word of God, the stronger faith becomes:

Joshua 1:8 This book of the law shall not depart out your mouth; but thou shalt meditate therein day and night, that thou mayest observe to do according to all that is written therein: for then thou shalt make thy way prosperous, and then thou shalt have good success.

Psalm 1:1-3 Blessed is the man that walketh not in the counsel of the ungodly, nor standeth in the way of sinners, nor sitteth in the seat of the scornful. But his delight is in the law of the Lord; and in his law doth he meditate day and night. And he shall be like a tree planted by the rivers of water, that bringeth forth fruit in his season; his leaf also shall not wither; and whatsoever he doeth shall prosper.

Romans 10:17 So then faith cometh by hearing, and hearing by the word of God.

II Peter 1:19 We have also a more sure word of prophecy; whereunto ye do well that ye take heed, as unto a light that shineth in a dark place, until the day dawn, and the day star arise in your hearts.

You will not become a Faith Giant overnight, have patience to let faith grow. Hence, Hebrews 6:12 tells us - Through faith and patience we inherit the promises of God.

Doctrine of Baptisms

Ephesians 4:5 states: "There is one Lord, one faith, and one baptism." Like a seven-faceted diamond whose emerald effervescence slowly spins in sacred suspension - there are seven baptisms in the New Testament which work together as one, which we experience as we are Going onto Perfection in the presence of God. These seven baptisms are amazingly more easily understood with their integration in the Tabernacle of Moses - explained in the following chapter. For now, they are listed in the order that we can experience them:

The Baptism into Repentance: (Acts 13:23-24) God according to his promise raised unto Israel a Saviour, Jesus: When John had first preached before his coming the baptism of repentance to all the people of Israel.

The Baptism into Water: (Luke 3:16) John answered, saying unto them all, I baptize you with water; but one mightier than I cometh, the latchet of whose shoes I am not worthy to unloose: he shall baptize you with the Holy Ghost and with fire.

The Baptism into the Holy Spirit: (Luke 3:16)

The Baptism into Fire: (Luke 3:16)

The Baptism in the Body: (I Corinthians 12:13) For by one spirit we are all baptized into one body, whether Jews or Gentiles, bond or free; and have been all made to drink into one spirit.

The Baptism into Death: (Romans 6:4) Therefore we are buried with him by baptism into death that like as Christ was raised up from the dead by the glory of the Father, even so we also should walk in newness of life.

The Baptism into the Cloud: (I Corinthians 10:1-2) Moreover, brethren, I would not that ye should be ignorant, how that all our fathers were under the cloud, and all passed through the sea; And were all baptized unto Moses in the cloud and in the sea.

Laying on of Hands

As we experience the Baptisms, the power of God will become increasingly evident in our life. We will watch miracles take place as we lay our hands on others and watch them receive healing, just as Jesus did:

Habakkuk 3:4 And his brightness was as the light; he had horns coming out of his hand: and there was the hiding place of his power.

We are now the Body of Christ in the earth, the Lord will work through his body (our hands) and manifest His power to heal others.

Matthew 10:7-8 And as ye go, preach, saying, The kingdom of heaven is at hand. Heal the sick, cleanse the lepers, raise the dead, cast out devils: freely ye have received, freely give.

Mark 16:17-18 And these signs shall follow them that believe; In my name shall they cast out devils; they shall speak with new tongues; They shall take up serpents; and if they drink any deadly thing, it shall not hurt them; they shall lay hands on the sick, and they shall recover.

Acts 5:12 And by the hands of the apostles were many signs and wonders wrought among the people.

This may seem strange to some - I believe we can lay our hands on our pets if they are not feeling well, lay hands on our checkbook if our finances are suffering, and even lay hands on our cars if they are not running properly. With God all things are possible, Jesus said - According to your faith be it unto you (Matthew 9:29).

The Resurrection of the Dead

Even though miracles, signs, and wonders are what we can experience in the presence of God, it is not the grand finale in actualizing the power of God in our lives. Jesus said, "Behold, I cast out devils, and I do cures today and tomorrow, and on the third day I shall be perfected" (Luke 13:32). We are now in the Third Day from when Jesus walked the earth - we are in the early stages of the Third Millennium. "One day with Lord is as a thousand years, and a thousand years as one day" (II Peter 3:8).

We have seen miracles take place in various ministries, however, we are now in the time that the Lord is revealing to us - Go onto Perfection (Hebrews 6:1), that we can be perfect even as our Father in heaven is perfect (Matthew 5:48). This perfection includes being raised into the death-less presence of God, where this mortal puts on immortality (I Corinthians 15:53).

Though the resurrection life can be in our spirit, it ascends slowly within our soul as we sow to the spirit. If we do not continue sowing to the spirit, we remain in the realm of death which leads to physical death. The Apostle Paul wrote of this reality in Romans 7:24, "O wretched man that I am! Who shall deliver me from the body of this death?" Here are various scriptures revealing that Christians are considered dead, until this corruption puts on incorruption:

Ephesians 5:14 Awake you who sleep and arise from the dead that Christ may give thee light.

Philippians 3:10-12 That I may know him, and the power of his resurrection, and the fellowship of his sufferings, being made conformable to his death; If by any means I might attain unto the resurrection of the dead.

I Timothy 5:6 But she that liveth in pleasure is dead while she liveth.

Revelation 3:1 And unto the angel of the church in Sardis write; These things saith he that hath the seven Spirits of God, and the seven stars; I know thy works, that thou hast a name that thou livest, and art dead.

The possibility of immortality now on earth through Jesus Christ will be expounded upon in Chapter Eleven – Imagining Immortality.

The Judgment of the Ages

Note: Most Bibles on the market currently read Eternal Judgment, however, if the Greek is properly translated it reads as above.

The final element of the Doctrine of Christ will be realized as Jesus is being glorified in us from glory to glory. The Light of Life exhibited in us will judge all things of death and darkness. Jesus said: This is the judgment, that light is come (John 3:19).

The prophet Isaiah spoke of this time: Arise shine; for thy light is come, and the glory of the Lord is risen upon thee. For, behold, the darkness shall cover the earth, and gross darkness the people: but the Lord shall arise upon thee, and his glory shall be seen upon thee. And the Gentiles shall come to thy light, and kings to the brightness of thy rising (Isaiah 60:1-3).

Throughout the endless horizons of eternity, those who have ascended into the illumination of the light of the presence of Jesus Christ, will rule the nations with a rod of iron in truth and righteousness. The following are a small portion of passages which signify this time:

Isaiah 63:12 And they shall call them, The holy people, The redeemed of the Lord: and thou shalt be called, Sought out, A city not forsaken.

Joel (Chapter Two)

Romans 8:19 For the earnest expectation of the

creation waiteth for the manifestation of the sons of God.

Jude 14-15 And Enoch also, the seventh from Adam, prophesied of these saying, Behold, the Lord cometh with ten thousands of his saints (the Greek reads, The Lord cometh in myriads of himself). To execute judgment upon all, and to convince all that are ungodly among them of all their ungodly deeds which they have ungodly committed, and of all their hard speeches which ungodly sinners have spoken against him.

Revelation 2:26-27 And he that overcometh, and keepeth my words unto the end, to him will I give power over the nations. And he shall rule them with a rod of iron; as vessels of a potter shall they be broken to shivers: even as I received of my Father.

Interpreting the Bible Spiritually

The Bible is a spiritual book inspired by the Holy Spirit for our spiritual growth. However, from the time I became a Christian at the age of 15 until I was 26, I was living in oblivion; lost in the passivest dream, wondering:

When will Jesus return?
When is the Rapture?
When will Armageddon take place?
Is so-and-so the Anti-Christ?
What are we having for dinner at the Marriage Supper of the Lamb?

While I was dreaming, I was listening to many of the

preachers on satellite and cable television, reading their books, and listening to their tapes, until I realized I was listening to those that Jesus warned us of in Luke 17:23: And they shall say to you, See here; or, see there: go not after them, nor follow them.

My current view of the Last Days is this: Yes, we are living in the Last Days – The Last Days of Babylon, The Last Days of ministries that are not preaching the Doctrine of Christ and Going onto Perfection, The Last Days of churches and world-wide ministries that preach Eternal Damnation, The Last Days of the Unspiritual Interpretations of the Bible, The Last Days of the Uncensored Gospel, and so forth.

What is the underlying theme of the Bible - the ultimate intention of God for our lives? Without hesitation, the answer is: To pursue God with all of our heart and mind that we may be flooded with the fullness of his presence - Going onto Perfection. Anything less than this - is Death.

Now and then we are warned of spiritualizing the Bible. My first reaction is, I hope they are not carnalizing the scripture. In 1993, I was being interviewed on a small AM Christian radio show in Minnesota. The interviewer asked me: I suppose you're going to give us the spiritual interpretation. My response was – "Well, hopefully it won't be the unspiritual interpretation." He gave me a blankstare for a moment, then we began to laugh.

The Bible is a transcendental masterpiece addressing various levels of spiritual growth. It can be interpreted many ways: figuratively, historically, literally, metaphorically, or, spiritually. In my view, our first inclination is to understand the spiritual interpretation – what is God telling us right now, that can assist us in moving continually deeper into the sweet repose of His immortal presence? The subsequent revelations maintain this view:

John 6:63 My words are spirit and they are life.

Romans 8: 5-6 For they that are after the flesh do mind the things of the flesh; but they that are after the Spirit mind the things of the Spirit. To be carnally minded is death, to be spiritually minded is life and peace.

I Corinthians 2:13-14 We speak not in words which mans wisdom teacheth, but which the Holy Ghost teacheth; comparing spiritual things with spiritual. But the natural man receiveth not the things of the Spirit of God: for they are foolishness unto him: neither can he know them, because they are spiritually discerned.

I Corinthians 3:1 Brethren, I could not speak unto you as unto spiritual, but as unto carnal, even as unto babes in Christ.

Colossians 1:9 Be filled with the knowledge of his will in all wisdom and spiritual understanding.

Grand Designs
Album: Power Windows

A to B –
Different degrees…

So much style without substance
So much stuff without style
It's hard to recognize the real thing
It comes along once in a while

Like a rare and precious metal
Beneath a ton of rock
It takes some time and trouble
To separate from the stock
You sometimes have to listen to
A lot of useless talk

Shapes and forms
Against the norms –
Against the run of the mill
Swimming against the stream
Life in two dimensions
Is a mass production scheme

So much poison in power
The principles get left out
So much mind on the matter
The spirit gets forgotten about

Like a righteous inspiration
Overlooked in haste
Like a teardrop in the ocean
A diamond in the waste
Some world-views are spacious –
And some are merely spaced

Against the run of the mill
Static as it seems
We break the surface tension
With our wild kinetic dreams
Curves and lines –
Of grand designs…

CHAPTER SEVEN

The Tabernacle of Moses: The Pattern of Spiritual Growth

And thine ears shall hear a word behind thee saying, This is the way, walk ye in it, when ye turn to the right hand, and when ye turn to the left.
Isaiah 30:21

The Path of Perfection

The true index of knowing if someone is really teaching you Biblical Truth, is to recognize if they are clarifying the different horizons we encounter on the road of our spiritual evolution. The Biblical road map to our ultimate spiritual destination is the Tabernacle of Moses.

It's one thing to know what the six principles of the Doctrine of Christ are, it is another thing to teach and believe them correctly according to the spiritual framework supernaturally crystallized in the Tabernacle. Before this chapter is completed, I will attempt to clarify the sublime synchronicity of the Doctrine of Baptisms and The Tabernacle of Moses.

Psalm 103:7 Israel knew his acts, Moses knew his ways.

It is the will of God that we all come into the unity of the faith and of the knowledge of the Son of God (Ephesians 4:13). To demonstrate the resolute nature of God in this matter of the Tabernacle of Moses as it relates to our spiritual growth, take time to read these passages in their full context:

Exodus 25:8-22 And let them make me a sanctuary; that I may dwell among them. According to all that I shew thee, after the pattern of the tabernacle. And there I will meet thee, and I will commune with thee from above the mercy seat.

Ezekiel 43:7-12 Thou son of man, shew the house to the house of Israel, let them measure the pattern. This is the law of the house; Upon the top of the mountain the whole limit thereof round about shall be most holy. Behold this is the law of the house.

Hebrews 8:5 The example and shadow of heavenly things as Moses was admonished of God when he was about to make the tabernacle: for, See, saith he, that thou make all things according to the pattern shewed to thee in the mount.

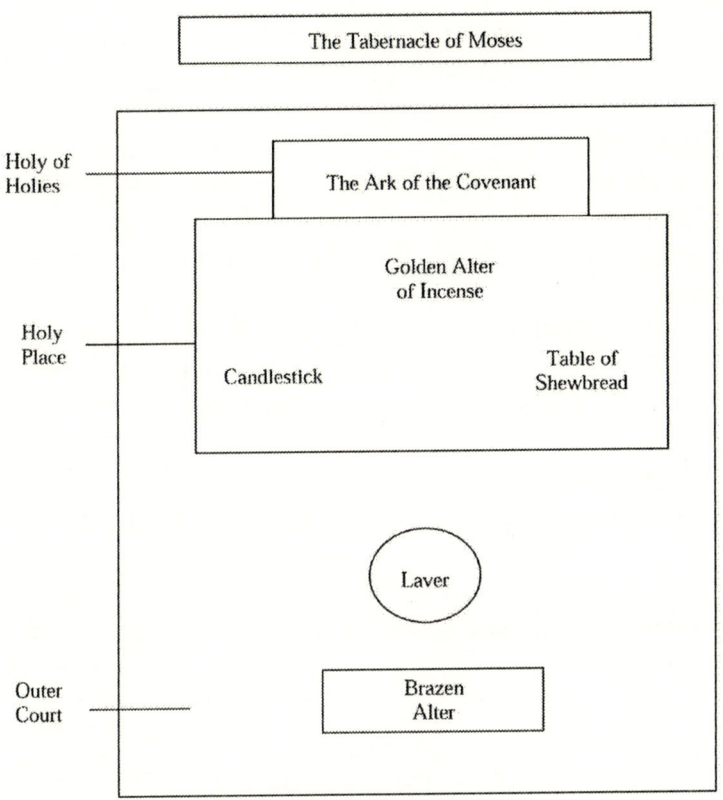

The three courts of the Tabernacle are a natural pattern for us to understand the will of God in moving us forward - staying linear rather than nonlinear, in our spiritual ascension into the presence of God. When a person is Born Again, their spirit is instantly illuminated with the Light of Life. The next experience, the salvation of the soul, and finally the body, is a progressive manifestation of the Spirit of God, realized as we journey into the Seven Sacred Spheres – the Seven Baptisms:

Outer Court
Brazen Alter = Baptism into Repentance.
The Laver = Baptism into Water.

The Holy Place
The Candlestick = Baptism into the Holy Spirit and Baptism into Fire.
The Table of Shewbread = Baptism into the Body and Baptism into Death.
The Golden Alter of Incense = All these Baptisms combined are represented in the Alter of Incense which typifies our prayers unto God (Revelation 5:8).

The Holy of Holies
The Ark of the Covenant = The Baptism into the Cloud.

The following is a brief description of what we experience with each Baptism:

Baptism into Repentance
Acts 13:23-24

In Old Testament times, the priests of Israel would shed the blood of bulls and goats at the **Brazen Alter** for the atonement of the sins of the people. This was a foreshadowing of the shedding of the blood of Jesus for each of us. When we simply call upon the name of the Lord for salvation, we can know that his blood has instantly evaporated our sin.

Romans 10:9-13 If thou shalt confess with thy mouth the Lord Jesus, and shalt believe in thine heart that God hath raised him from the dead, thou shalt be saved. For with the heart man believeth unto righteousness; and with the mouth confession is made unto salvation. For the scripture saith, Whosoever believeth on him shall not be ashamed. For there is no difference between the Jew and the Greek: for the same Lord over all is rich unto all that call upon him. For whosoever shall call upon the name of the Lord shall be saved.

I John 1:9 If we confess our sins, he is faithful and just to forgive us our sins, and cleanse us from all unrighteousness.

Baptism into Water
Luke 3:16

When the priests of Israel were finished with the bloody sacrifices, they moved to **The Laver** to wash themselves. This is a figure for Water Baptism. The first few years of my life with Jesus, I worried at times that if I was not water baptized, I might go to hell. I do believe as others say: Water Baptism is an outward sign of an inward work. John the Baptist said: "I baptize you with water, but Jesus will baptize you with the Holy Ghost and Fire." Even Jesus, when He was thirty years old, ready to begin his ministry, was water baptized, after which the Holy Spirit descended upon him as a dove (Luke 3:21-23).

My favorite episode of water baptism in the New Testament is when Philip baptized the treasurer for Candace, the Queen of Ethiopia. He was a savvy political operator in charge of all her treasure. After the man believed on Jesus for salvation, he was water baptized. After which, Philip was translated by the Spirit of God from Gaza to Azotus (Acts 8:27-40).

You don't need to go to a church to be baptized in water.

You can baptize yourself in the bathtub, swimming pool, or hot-tub - whatever. All that matters, is that you are sincere with Jesus. Water baptism is not something you need to do to be accepted or loved by the Lord. It's an outward sign that you have made Jesus your Lord and Saviour, not for others, but for yourself. Jesus said: "It is written in your law, that the testimony of two men is true. I am one that bear witness of myself, and the Father that sent me beareth witness of me" (John 8:17-18). If you don't have a tub, go into a shower - and pray to the Lord: "Lord Jesus, you are my Lord and Saviour, and by the testimony of two witnesses, you and I, I now baptize myself in your sacred Holy name. Amen."

The other spiritual experience we encounter at **The Laver** is being washed with the water of the word of God (Ephesians 5:26). We need to be brainwashed - to have our minds cleansed from the illusions of darkness that have encroached themselves on us in the world:

John 15:3 Now ye are clean, through the word, which I have spoken to you.

John 15:7-8 If ye abide in me, and my words abide in you, ye shall ask what ye will, and it shall be done unto you. Herein is my Father glorified that ye bear much fruit; so shall ye be my disciples.

Romans 12:2 And be not conformed to this world: but be ye transformed by the renewing of your mind, that ye may prove what is that good, and acceptable, and perfect will of God.

Colossians 3:16 Let the word of Christ dwell in you richly in all wisdom; teaching and admonishing one another in psalms and hymns and spiritual songs, singing with grace in your hearts to the Lord.

Psalm 63:5-6 My soul shall be satisfied as with marrow and fatness; and my mouth shall praise thee with joyful lips. When I remember thee upon my bed, and meditate on thee in the night watches.

Psalm 119: (All of it)

I Timothy 4:15 Meditate upon these things; give thyself wholly to them; that thy profiting may appear to all.

Baptism in the Holy Spirit and Fire.

Once the priests had washed themselves at the Laver, they entered into the Holy Place, and lit **The Candlestick -** also known as the Menorah. This is a beautiful depiction of the third and fourth baptisms - The Baptism in the Holy Spirit and Baptism into Fire. Many churches don't believe in the Baptism in the Holy Spirit, they are unbelieving believers, which is why those churches are dead, and have no power, or manifestations of the Holy Spirit of signs and wonders. You don't feel the presence of the Lord there very much. Timothy wrote of these types of religious systems: Having a form of godliness, but denying the power thereof: from such turn away (II Timothy 3:5).

I grew up in a Protestant church. After I became a Christian, my friends in our church youth group wondered about me: why is the guy who usually is firing everyone up to play Frisbee football or volleyball, now wanting to have Bible studies all the time? A few years later, our family moved on to another church. One church we attended had a sign on the wall that said - A church that is alive is worth the drive.

Luke 24:49 And, behold, I send the promise of my Father upon you (The Holy Spirit): but tarry ye in the city of Jerusalem, until ye be endued with power from on high.

Jesus told His disciples to not begin a ministry until they had been empowered by the Holy Spirit. Jesus did not require four years of college and four more years of seminary to be in His ministry. Based on the scripture above, there should be fewer churches around the world.

Acts 1:8 But ye shall receive power, after that the Holy Ghost is come upon you: and ye shall be witnesses unto me both in Jerusalem, and in all Judea, and in Samaria, and unto the uttermost part of the earth.

Acts 2: 1-4 And when the day of Pentecost was fully come, they were all with one accord in one place. And suddenly there came a sound from heaven as of a rushing mighty wind, and it filled all the house where they were sitting. And there appeared unto them cloven tongues like as of fire, and it sat upon each of them. And they were all filled with the Holy Ghost, and began to speak with tongues, as the Spirit gave them utterance.

I heard one preacher say: "Getting baptized in the Holy Spirit is like buying a pair of running shoes – you get the tongues to." The purpose of Praying in Tongues, or Praying in the Spirit is revealed in the following passage:

Romans 8:26-28 Likewise the Spirit also helpeth our infirmities: for we know not what we should pray for as we ought: but the Spirit itself maketh intercession for us with groanings which cannot be uttered. And he that searcheth the hearts knoweth what is the mind of the Spirit, because he maketh intercession for the saints according to the will of God. And we know that all things work together for good to them that love God, to them who are the called according to his purpose.

The purpose or will of God is always perfect. The way to prime the pump, for the outflow of the perfect will of God into our lives, is through praying in the Spirit. At times this can actualize into literal groanings. Isaiah 66:8b As soon as Zion travailed, she brought forth children.

NOTE: There will be more thoughts and scriptures on Praying in the Holy Spirit in Chapter Fifteen- The Queen of the South.

For me personally, the Baptism in the Holy Spirit and Baptism into Fire are synonymous occurrences. The more I pray in the Spirit, the more I feel the fire of God burning in me, evaporating desires to live in the flesh, or do anything which grieves the Holy Spirit.

Matthew 3:11-12 I (John the Baptist) indeed baptize you with water unto repentance: but he that cometh after me is mightier than I, whose shoes I am not worthy to bear: he shall baptize you with the Holy Ghost and fire: Whose fan is in his had, and he will thoroughly purge his floor (in His Temple, which we are (Hebrews 3:6), and gather wheat into the garner; but he will burn up the chaff with unquenchable fire.

The Lord is faithful and true to do His work of holiness in us, which he typifies by fire. It is in these trials by fire that we are refined in the Spirit. Isaiah 48:10 states: Behold, I have refined thee, but not with silver; I have chosen thee in the furnace of affliction.

The Baptism into the Body

After the priests lit the Candlestick, they moved over to **The Table of Shewbread** and partook of twelve loaves of Unleavened Bread. This typifies the Baptism into the Body and Baptism into Death. Jesus is the Bread of Life. He has promised to provide for us our daily bread (Matthew 6:11) - our daily dose of His presence, if we shall seek Him. They that seek Him, shall find Him (Matthew 7:7). Jesus said in John 6:51 – I am the living bread which came down from heaven: if any man eat this bread, he shall live for ever: and that bread that I will give is my flesh, which I will give for the life of the world.

> I Corinthians 12:13 For by one Spirit we are all baptized into one body, whether Jews or Gentiles, bond or free; and have been all made to drink into one Spirit."

I am not interested in eating the bread of Babylon, or, being Baptized into the Body of Babylon. We are to be Baptized into Zion - Going onto Perfection, into the immortal realms of His presence. Jesus said in John 6:58 This is the bread which came down from heaven: not as your fathers did eat manna, and are dead: he that eateth of this bread shall live forever.

I have dedicated an entire chapter to this subject – Chapter Nine: Meeting Jesus Outside The Box

The Baptism into Death

Romans 6:4 Therefore we are buried with him by baptism into death: that like as Christ was raised up from the dead by the glory of the Father, even so we also should walk in newness of life."

As we grow into the presence of the Lord, the carnal nature of our soul = The Old Man, dies - as the New Man ascends within our soul (Ephesians 4:22). The following scriptures will illuminate this experience:

Mark 8:34-36 Whosoever will come after me, let him deny himself, and take up his cross, and follow me. For whosoever will save his <u>life</u> (The Greek word is Psuche = Soul) shall lose it; but whosoever shall lose his life (Soul) for my sake and the gospel's, the same shall save it. For what shall it profit a man, if he shall gain the whole world, and lose his own <u>soul</u>?" (The translators got it right on that one)

I Corinthians 15:31 I protest by your rejoicing which I have in Christ Jesus our Lord, I die daily.

Revelation 12:11 And they overcame him (The Old Man = The Devil) by the blood of the Lamb, and by the word of their testimony; <u>and they loved not their lives (Souls) unto the death.</u>

Revelation 2:11 He that hath an ear, let him hear what the Spirit saith unto the churches; He that over-cometh shall not be hurt of the second death.

Revelation 21:8 But the fearful, and unbelieving,

and the abominable, and murderers, and whoremon-
gers, and sorcerers, and idolaters, and all liars, shall
have their part in the lake of fire which burneth with
fire and brimstone: which is the second death.

The Second Death is the death of Death. The death of
the Old Man with his carnal mind which is death (Romans
8:6). In order to understand this more clearly, read Chapter
Ten - Hell: The Cruel Illusion.

The Baptism into the Cloud
I Corinthians 10:2

Not all of the priests entered the Holy of Holies where
the **Ark of the Covenant** was, only the High Priest. So
also, if we grow up into the head which is Christ
(Ephesians 4:15) we shall enter the deathless realm of the
Holy of Holies, we shall be caught up into the cloud of His
presence. I do believe in the Rapture, this is it: Salvation -
Spirit, Soul, and Body.

Exodus 25:22a And there I will meet with thee, and I
will commune with thee from above the mercy seat.

Leviticus 16:2b For I will appear in the cloud above
the mercy seat.

I Thessalonians 4:17 Then we which are alive and
remain, shall be caught up together with them in the
clouds, to meet the Lord in the air: and so shall we
ever be with the Lord.

Keep in mind, all Bible teaching as it relates to our spiritual growth, should coincide with the Doctrine of Christ

and the pattern of the Tabernacle of Moses.

For more detail concerning the Coming of the Lord, please read Chapter Ten: The Second Ascension.

The Tabernacle of David

And David made him houses in the city of David, and prepared a place for the ark of God and pitched for it a tent. Then David said, None ought to carry the ark of God but the Levites: for them hath the Lord chosen to carry the ark of God, and to minister unto him for ever (I Chronicles 15:1-2).

In that day will I raise up the tabernacle of David that is fallen, and close up the breaches thereof; and I will raise up his ruins, and I will build it as in the days of old (Amos 9:11).

And to this agree the word of the prophets; as it is written, After this I will return, and will build again the tabernacle of David, which is fallen down; and I will build again the ruins thereof, and I will set it up (Acts 15:15-16).

The Tabernacle of David was a humble tent pitched on Mount Zion that contained only the Ark of the Covenant, which represents the opening into the Immortal Spheres of the Presence of God, flooding us from within. We are now in the endless season of the Tabernacle of David. The Alpha and the Omega announced in Revelation 3:7 - And to the angel of the church of Philadelphia write; These things saith he that is holy, he that is true, he that hath the key of David, he that openeth, and no man shutteth; and shutteth, and no man openeth.

The Key of David is a symbol for the written word of God, which opens the door of our minds to the celestial reality of entering the Holy of Holies and becoming an Ark of the Covenant for the presence of the Lord to dwell upon - to manifest His Glory in the Earth.

II Samuel 17:22 Then David arose, and all the people who were him, and they passed over Jordan by the morning light: there lacked not one of them that was not gone over Jordan.

Isaiah 62:1-3 For Zion's sake will I not hold my peace, and for Jerusalem's sake I will not rest, until the righteousness thereof go forth as brightness, and the salvation thereof as a lamp that burneth. And the Gentiles shall see thy righteousness, and all kings thy glory: and thou shalt be called by my new name, which the mouth of the Lord shall name. Thou shalt also be a crown of glory in the hand of the Lord, and a royal diadem in the hand of thy God.

We are now in the hour when the truth of the Ark of the Covenant is being made known. Those that do not receive the message shall not have the Power and the Glory. The Old Testament speaks of our time by types and shadows. I Peter 1:12 records of the prophets: Unto whom it was revealed, that not unto themselves, but unto us did they minister the things, which are now reported unto you by them that have preached the gospel unto you with the Holy Ghost sent down from heaven; which things the angels desire to look into.

Hence, the following scriptures speak of this present time. Read them in their full context, there are paraphrased here:

I Samuel 4:15-22 Now Eli (the High Priest of Israel) was ninety-eight years old; his eyes were dim, that he could not see (the state of the religious systems today). And it came to pass, when Eli heard the Ark was taken by the Philistines, he fell backwards, broke his neck and died. His daughter in law

Phinehas had a child who she named Ichabod, saying, The glory is departed from Israel: because the ark of God was taken. The glory is departed from Israel: for the ark of God is taken. (She said it twice, back to back).

II Samuel 15:6-29 So Absalom (David's son) stole the hearts of the men of Israel. They went in their simplicity and knew nothing. Zadok therefore and Abiathar carried the ark of God again to Jerusalem: and they tarried there.

Here we have a perfect picture of what is going on today. Religious entities of all kinds are stealing the hearts of believers away from the truth of God to obtain their true spiritual inheritance which is found in the Doctrine of Christ and Going onto Perfection.

Many today will not study the meat of the word of God, they say - I just like it simple.

They remind me of the men of Israel that followed Absalom. Hosea 4: 6 decrees - My people are destroyed for a lack of knowledge: because thou hast rejected knowledge, I will also reject thee, that thou shalt be no priest to me: seeing thou hast forgotten the law of thy God, I will also forget thy children.

Cinderella Man
Album: A Farewell To Kings

A modest man from Mandrake
Travelled rich to the city
He had a need to discover
A use for his newly-found wealth

Because he was human
Because he had goodness
Because he was moral
They called him insane

Delusions of grandeur
Visions of splendour
A manic depressive
He walks in the rain

Eyes wide open
Heart undefended
Innocence untarnished...

Cinderella Man
Doing what you can
They can't understand
What it means

Cinderella Man
Hang on to your plans
Try as they might
They cannot steal your dreams

In the betrayal of his love he awakened
To face a world of cold reality
And a look in the eyes of the hungry
Awakened him to what he could do

He held up his riches
To challenge the hungry
Purposeful motion
For one so insane

They tried to fight him
Just couldn't beat him
This manic depressive
Who walks in the rain

CHAPTER EIGHT

The Order of Melchizedek

Don't slip on the Royal Robe – put it on.
- Jerry Marcom

Jesus Christ did not come to establish a religion called - Christianity. Jesus came to establish the Kingdom of God (Mark 1:14-15) = His Government (Isaiah 9:6) = His Kingdom of Priests (Exodus 19:6) = His Royal Priesthood (I Peter 2:9). This Royal Priesthood is called - The Order of Melchizedek.

Various spiritual communities and organizations, have found the name Melchizedek to be in vogue. They use this title in their rhetoric in an effort to legitimize themselves. However, not all of them glorify Jesus Christ as our only Saviour, Lord, and King.

Let there be no misconception: The following three recitals are what the Order of Melchizedek - The Royal Priesthood of Jesus Christ, believes and teaches, with no reservations for the opinions and traditions of men:

1. They believe and partake of the Tree of Life by acknowledging that everything is happening for a reason and His name is Jesus Christ - the High Priest after the Order of Melchizedek, who has all power in heaven and in earth. Therefore, they do not eat from the Tree of the Knowledge of Good and Evil.

2. They believe and teach the Restoration of All Things, which is the fulfillment of the Abrahamic Covenant = The True Gospel (Acts 3:19-26).

3. They believe, teach, and boldly vaticinate the Doctrine of Christ and Going onto Perfection (Hebrews 6:1-2), which is the salvation of our spirit, soul, and body. They seek not to please men, but seek only to please the Lord Jesus Christ in truth and righteousness.

Melchizedek: A Mystical Mystery

Who on earth is Melchizedek? The answer is found in Hebrews 7:1-3:

For this Melchizedek, king of Salem, priest of the most high God, who met Abraham returning from the slaughter of the kings, and blessed him. To whom also Abraham gave a tenth part of all, being by interpretation King of Righteousness, and after that also King of Salem, which is King of peace; without father, without mother, without descent, having no beginning of days, nor end of life, but made like unto the Son of God; abideth a priest continually.

To pinpoint it: Melchizedek is Jesus Christ = The Word of God. There is no King of Righteousness or King of Peace, other than the King of Kings and Lord of Lords - the High Priest of our profession (Revelation 19:16 and Hebrews 3:1). In Genesis 14:18, the Alpha and Omega discreetly stepped out of the spiritual stratosphere as an Immortal Theophany: a manifestation of the divine. The following oracles speak of Melchizedek:

Genesis 14:18-19 And Melchizedek king of Salem brought forth bread and wine: and he was the priest of the most high God. And he blessed him, and said, Blessed be Abram of the most high God, possessor of heaven and earth.

Psalm 110:4 The Lord hath sworn, and will not repent, Thou art a priest for ever after the order of Melchizedek.

Hebrews 5:6 As he saith also in another place, Thou art a priest for ever after the order Melchizedek.

Hebrews 5:8-10 Though he were a Son, yet he learned obedience by the things which he suffered; And being made perfect, he became the author of eternal salvation unto all them that obey him; Called of God an high priest after the order of Melchizedek.

Hebrews 6:20 Wither the forerunner is for us entered, even Jesus, made an high priest for ever after the order of Melchizedek.

Hebrews 7:11 If therefore perfection were by the Levitical priesthood, (for under it the people received the law,) what further need was there that another priest should rise after the order of Melchizedek, and not be called after the order of Aaron?

Hebrews 7:14-17 For it is evident that our Lord

sprang out of Judah; of which tribe Moses space nothing concerning priesthood. And it is yet far more evident: for that after the similitude of Melchizedek there arises another priest, Who is made, not after the law of carnal commandment, but after the power of an endless life. For he testified, Thou art a priest for ever after the order of Melchizedek.

The Real Israel and the True Zion

Many Christians believe that they must firmly support natural Israel. They have been taught Jesus will make His landing there at His coming. Such deception could be avoided by merely reading the Bible with a spiritual mind. This section may stir up some controversy in the minds of those who do not agree that the Bible is the final authority when discussing spiritual truth.

The following holy oracles of fire shall burn away the dross of deception, and reveal to us that our attention is not to be focused on the natural nation of Israel, any more than any other ethnic group. These scriptures having nothing to do with creating conditions of anti-Semitism. Alternately, they are being provided to generate the atmosphere of being Pro-Jesus Christ = Pro-The Word of God:

Zechariah 2:4 Jerusalem shall be inhabited as towns without walls for the multitude of men and cattle therein.

Zechariah is prophesying of the New Jerusalem, the saints of God that make up the Royal Priesthood of Jesus Christ, spread throughout the nations of the earth.

Matthew 3:19 Think not to say within yourselves, We have Abraham as our Father: For God is able of these stones to raise up children unto Abraham.

Jesus spoke this to the Scribes and Pharisees who were riding off the laurels of the Old Covenant, thinking they were more special than the Gentiles.

John 8:39 If ye were Abraham's children, ye would do the works of Abraham.

Jesus said this also to the Scribes and Pharisees, the leaders of Israel, who were seeking to kill Jesus. (John 8:37)

Romans 2:28-29 For he is not a Jew, which is one outwardly; neither is that circumcision, which is outward in the flesh: But he is a Jew, which is one inwardly; and circumcision is that of the heart, in the spirit, and not in the letter; whose praise is not of men, but of God.

This is the most unfiltered verse in this context. Because it is so clear, many preachers will not boldly proclaim it. To me, a man or woman of God = A man or woman of truth. Many fear men more than they fear God. They acquiesce in fear, afraid people will label them anti-Semitic. Jesus is strolling through the land as a lion; as a leopard by the way in this hour, observing those that will preach His word, not playing paddy-cake by preaching what the masses want to hear. (Hosea 13:7).

Romans 9:6-8 For they are not all Israel, which are of Israel. Neither, Because they are the seed of Abraham, are they all children: but, In Isaac shall thy seed be called. That is, They which are the children of the flesh, these are not the children of God: but the children of the promise are counted for the seed.

This verse also unmistakably spells out that all those of natural Israel - are not the true Israel.

Galatians 3:29 And if ye be Christ's then are ye Abraham's seed, and heirs according to the promise.

Galatians 4: 25-26 For this Agar is mount Sinai in Arabia, and answereth to Jerusalem which now is, and is in bondage with her children. But the Jerusalem which is above is free, which is the mother of us all.

Galatians 4:30-31 Nevertheless what saith the scripture? Cast out the bondwomen and her son: for the son of the bondwomen shall not be heir with the son of the freewomen. So then, brethren, we are not children of the bondwomen, but of the free.

To receive the full impact of the preceding scripture, the whole Fourth chapter of Galatians should be examined.

Galatians 6:16 (Amplified Bible) Peace and mercy are upon the true Israel of God.

Ephesians 2:11-13 Wherefore remember, that ye being in time past Gentiles in the flesh, who are called the Uncircumcision by that which is called the Circumcision in the flesh made by hands; That at that time ye were without Christ, being aliens from the commonwealth of Israel, and strangers from the covenants of promise, having no hope and without God in the world: But now in Christ Jesus ye who sometimes were far off are made nigh by the blood of Christ.

This verse is clear again. The commonwealth of Israel, are those who have been made nigh by the blood of Christ.

Philippians 3:3 We are the circumcision, which worship God in the spirit, and rejoice in Christ Jesus, and have no confidence in the flesh.

Hebrews 12:22-24 But ye are come (present tense) unto mount Zion, and unto the city of the living God, the heavenly Jerusalem, and to an innumerable company of angels, To the general assembly and church of the firstborn, which are written in heaven, and to God, the judge of all, and to the spirits of just men made perfect, And to Jesus the mediator of the new covenant, and to the blood of sprinkling, that speaketh better things than that of Abel.

Whether you live in New Zealand, China, Austria, South Africa, or wherever – if you have come to Christ, you have come to Mount Zion. Now it's time to start ascending Zion, by growing continually deeper into the presence of God.

James 1:1-3 James, a servant of God and of the Lord Jesus Christ, to the twelve tribes which are scattered abroad, greeting. My brethren, count it all joy when ye fall into divers temptations; Knowing this, that the trying of your faith worketh patience.

Here James, the brother of Jesus, addresses the body of Christ as the twelve tribes, we know this, in that he calls them, My brethren.

I Peter 2:9 But ye are a chosen generation, a royal priesthood, an holy nation, a peculiar people; that ye should shew forth the praises of him who hath called you out of darkness into his marvelous light.

In I Peter 1:1, I like how the Apostle Peter addresses the Royal Priesthood as - Strangers.When you mention to others that you are a priest in the Order of Melchizedek, which is the Royal Priesthood of Jesus Christ, they will think you are strange.

Revelation 2:9 I know the blasphemy of them that say they are Jews, and are not, but are the synagogue of Satan.

Whether we consider ourselves natural Jews or spiritual Jews - if we are not in obedience to the Lord Jesus Christ, we are of the synagogue of Satan. When Peter rebuked Jesus in Matthew 16:22-23, Jesus said unto Peter - Get thee behind me, Satan.

Revelation 3:9 Behold, I will make them of the synagogue of Satan, which say they are Jews, and are not, but do lie; behold, I will make them to come and worship before thy feet, and to know that I have loved thee.

Revelation 3:12-13 Him that overcometh will I make a pillar in the temple of my God, and he shall no more go out: and I will write upon him the name of my God, and the name of the city of my God, which is the New Jerusalem, which cometh down out of heaven from my God: and I will write upon him my new name. He that hath an ear, let him hear what the Spirit saith unto the churches.

Synonymous By Association

Within the Bible, the Spirit of God has inspired different spiritual names or phrases to uniquely characterize who we are in Jesus Christ on earth. All of us in the Body of Christ, are positionally called these names by the Spirit. As we grow deeper into the presence of Jesus, they will become experientially true:

The Kingdom of Priests (Exodus 19:6)

The Order of Melchizedek (Psalm 110:4 and Hebrews 5,6, and 7)

A very small remnant (Isaiah 1:9)

The Government (Isaiah 9:6)

The City of the Lord (Isaiah 60:14)

Priests of the Lord (Isaiah 61:6)

A Royal Diadem (Isaiah 62:3)

The Redeemed of the Lord, Sought out, A city not forsaken (Isaiah 62:12)

The Sons of Zadok (Ezekiel 48:11)

Zion (Joel chapter 2)

Saviors upon Zion (Obadiah 21)

The City of Truth (Zechariah 8:3)

The Queen of the South (Matthew 12:42 and Luke 11:31)

The Manifestation of the Sons of God (Romans 8:9)

The Glorious Church (Ephesians 5:27)

The Mighty Angels (II Thessalonians 1:7)

The Strangers (I Peter 1:1)

The Chosen Generation, Royal Priesthood, Holy Nation, and Peculiar People (I Peter 2:9)

The Seven Stars (Revelation 1:6 and 1:20)

The Seven Angels (Revelation 1:20)

The Overcomers (Revelation 2 and 3)

The New Jerusalem (Revelation 3:12 and 21:10-11)

Kings and Priests (Revelation 1:6 and 5:10)

The 144,000 (Revelation 14:3)

The Kings of the East (Revelation 16:12)

The Armies in Heaven on White Horses (Revelation 19:14)

The Bride (Revelation 19 and 21)

Red Barchetta
Album: Moving Pictures

My uncle has a country place, that no-one
knows about
He says it used to be a farm, before the
Motor Law
Sundays I elude the 'Eyes', and hop the
Turbine freight
To far outside the Wire, where my white-
haired uncle waits

Jump to the ground
As the Turbo slows to cross the borderline
Run like the wind,
As excitement shivers up and down my spine
Down in his barn
My uncle preserved for me, an old machine –
For fifty-odd years
To keep it as new has been his dearest dream

I strip away the old debris, that hides the
shining car
A brilliant red Barchetta, from a better,
vanished time
Fire up the willing engine, responding with
a roar!
Tires spitting gravel, I commit my weekly
crime...

Wind in my hair –
Shifting and drifting –
Mechanical music
Adrenaline surge –

Lee Janisson

Well-weathered leather
Hot metal and oil
The scented country air
The blur of the landscape
Every nerve aware

Suddenly, ahead of me, across the
mountainside
A gleaming alloy air-car shoots towards me,
two lanes wide
I spin around with shrieking tires, to run the
deadly race
Go screaming through the valley as another
joins the chase

Drive like the wind
Straining the limits of machine and man
Laughing out loud
With fear and hope, I've got a desperate plan

At the one-lane bridge
I leave the giants stranded
At the riverside
Race back to the farm
To dream with my uncle
At the fireside...

Inspired by 'A Nice Morning Drive' by Richard S. Foster

CHAPTER NINE

Meeting Jesus Outside the Box

Every Exit is an Entrance
- Unknown

I grew up in a small town with a population of around five-thousand people. There are five churches within a block of the house that I was raised in. Going to church every Sunday and on Christmas and Easter was our way of life, I look back with warm memories of the friends I made at our church. I still enjoy going there every Christmas Eve for the midnight candlelight service and meeting old faces. There is nothing more beautiful than an old European style sanctuary decorated with Christmas trees and wreathes - lit up with white lights, as the choir in the balcony sings - *O' Holy Night*, with snow falling softly outside the dimly-lit sapphire stained-glass windows.

At the same time, like many churches, the leadership of the church I was raised in, continues to not preach the Doctrine of Christ and Going Onto Perfection.

Ezekiel 34:2b Woe be to the shepherds of Israel that do feed themselves! Should not the shepherds of Israel feed the flocks?

Our relationship with Jesus is not about – Going to Church. Alternately, our relationship with Jesus is about – Going onto Perfection.

Seeking Him After Due Order

The Lord God made a breach upon us because we did not seek him after due order (I Chronicles 15:13).
The due order in which we are to seek the Lord Jesus Christ is based in the Doctrine of Christ and the pattern of our spiritual growth, clarified in the Tabernacle of Moses.

Isaiah 30:1 states: Woe to the rebellious children, saith the Lord, that take counsel, but not of me; and that cover with a covering, but not of my spirit, that they might add sin to sin.

The way most churches operate today is through a pastor or priest, and maybe an associate, who are subject to the Church Board that hired them. They love *the shade and the wage* (Job 7:2). This is out of sync with the Bible. The correct order is found in the following passages:

I Corinthians 12:28: And God hath set some in the church, first apostles, secondarily prophets, thirdly teachers, after that miracles, helps, governments, diversities of tongues.

Ephesians 4:11-13: And he gave some, apostles; and some, prophets; and some, evangelists; and some, pastors and teachers; For the perfecting of the saints, for the work of the ministry, for the edifying of the body of Christ: Till we all come in the unity of the faith, and of the knowledge of the Son of God, unto a perfect man, unto the measure of the stature of the fullness of Christ: That we henceforth be no more children, tossed to and fro, and carried about with every wind of doctrine, by the sleight of men, and cunning craftiness, whereby they lie in wait to deceive.

Generally speaking, the so-called Church these days, is spinning off to every extreme, far from being in the unity of the faith.

Why?

They are not preaching the Doctrine of Christ and Going onto Perfection (Hebrews 6:1-2). Ephesians 4 says, we have been given apostles, prophets, evangelists, pastors, and teachers UNTIL we come into the unity of the faith - unto a perfect man.

Once we realize that the ultimate intention of Jesus is for us to Go Onto Perfection, we no longer have any need for these type of ministries. In this hour, we need to have discernment in where the Spirit of God is taking His remnant - Out of the Church realm and into the realm of the Kingdom, not just positionally - but experientially. We see the truth of no longer needing the ministries of man high-lighted in I John 2:26-27:

These things have I written unto you concerning them that seduce you. But the anointing which ye have received of him abideth in you, and ye need not that any man teach you: but as the same anointing teacheth you of all things, and is truth, and is no lie, and even as it hath taught you, ye shall abide in him.

Romans 16:17 Now I beseech you, brethren, mark them which cause divisions and offenses contrary to the doctrine which ye have learned (The Doctrine of Christ); and avoid them.

Jesus rebuked the Church in Pergamos in Revelation 2:15 - So hast thou also them that hold the doctrine of the Nicolaitans, which thing I hate.

The name Nicolaitan, means - Victory over the people, the laity. Some preachers love to be fawned after, to be known as - Apostle, Evangelist, Pastor, Elder, Deacon, Bishop, God's Man of the Hour, or Doctor. When I see PhD behind a preacher's name, sometimes I wonder if it's an acronym for Post Hole Digger.

Isaiah 3:1-3 For, behold, the Lord, the Lord of hosts, doth take away from Jerusalem and from Judah the stay and the staff, the whole stay of bread, and the whole stay of water, The might man, and the man of war, the judge, and the prophet, and the prudent, and the ancient, The captain of fifty, and the honourable man, and the counselor, and the cunning artificer, and the eloquent orator. And I will give children to be their princes, and babes shall rule over them.

"Less has he, and many of the more same bevy that I know, that drossy age dotes on, that only have the tune of the times, an outward habit of encounter, a kind of yeasty collection which carries him through the most fanned and wintered opinions and do but blow them to their trial, the bubbles are out." - Hamlet.

Diotrephes and Demetrius

All who claim to speak for God can be categorized as a Diotrephes or a Demetrius. We find this in the Third Epistle of John:

Verse 9: I wrote unto the church: but Diotrephes, who loved to have preeminence among them, receiveth us not.

Verse 12: Demetrius hath good report of all men, and of the truth itself: yea, and we also bear record; and ye know that our record is true.

The Demetrius preachers in this era, boldly preach the truth of the Restoration of All Things, The Doctrine of Christ and Going onto Perfection. The Diotrephes preachers love to have power and influence over their people. They are as Adonijah who exalted himself to be king when David was on his death bed. But Zadok the priest and Nathan the prophet were not with him (I Kings 1: 1-5).

Forsaking the Assembly of Babylon

We would have healed Babylon, but she was not healed: forsake her, and let us go every one into his own country (Jeremiah 51:9).

Many preachers today, in an effort to elicit the empathy of their audience, to sustain church attendance, coax their congregations with Hebrews 10:25 - Not forsaking the assembling of ourselves together, as the manner of some is, but exhorting one another: and so much the more, as ye see the day approaching.

The Greek word for - assembling, is Episunagoge. Epi –

means, The highest form of. Sunagoge – means, Gathering together. This Greek word is found nowhere else in the New Testament. In the Book of Acts (4:31 and 11:26) it says - they *assembled together*. In both instances, the Greek word is Sunagoge, not Episunagoge.

The highest form of assembly is in Zion with Jesus, and others He places in our path with an affinity to - Go onto Perfection. These are the saints we are to exhort concerning the Day of the Lord approaching <u>in them.</u>

II Peter 1:19b proclaims: Ye do well that ye take heed, as unto a light that shineth in a dark place, until the day dawn, and the daystar arise in your hearts.

Jesus is the Daystar = The Bright and Morning Star (Revelation 22:16). Clear logic leads us to conclude that the Day of the Daystar = The Day of the Lord.

Coming out of Babylon

For those squeezing the limit of the literal interpretation of the Bible, the following section should be of intrigue. This section is based in Revelation 18:4 -

And I heard another voice from heaven, saying, Come out or her, my people, that ye be not partakers of her sins, and that ye receive not of her plagues.

This is spoken from the burning zone of the love of the Lord Jesus Christ. He is demanding that His true lovers (The Bride), are to come up hither, making the exit from the religious system of Babylon – the Great Whore that sitteth upon many waters which are peoples and multitudes, and nations, and tongues (Revelation 17:1 and15).

Isaiah 1:13 Bring no more vain oblations; incense is an abomination unto me; the new moons and Sabbaths, the calling of assemblies, I cannot away with, it is iniquity, even the solemn meeting.

Galatians 4:10-11 Ye observe days, and months, and times, and years. I am afraid of you, lest I have bestowed upon you labour in vain.

I Corinthians 11:17 Now in this that I declare unto you I praise you not, that ye come together not for the better, but for the worse.

Isolating Babylon

We don't want to be caught trolling for abstractions, this is the era to isolate who Babylon the Great Whore is:

Babylon does not preach – God works all things after the counsel of his own will (Ephesians 1:11). Rather, she eats from the Tree of the Knowledge of Good and Evil.

Babylon does not preach the Doctrine of Christ and Going on to Perfection (Hebrews 6:1-2). Rather, she entertains her audience, keeping them comfortable with no changes which induce spiritual growth. She is a whore - she needs to keep the cash flowing.

Babylon does not preach the Restoration of All Things = The Abrahamic Covenant = The True Gospel (Acts 3:19-26). Rather, she preaches the Restoration of Some Things: Some will go to heaven forever, and the rest will spend eternity in hell.

Babylon does not preach Immortality: Salvation - Spirit, Soul, and Body (I Thessalonians 5:23). Rather, she preaches a false Rapture, or, that we all must experience the Deep Six, that death is just a part of life.

Babylon absolutely does not preach - My People, Come Out of Babylon (Revelation 18:4). Rather, she is now arranging her next money–making maneuver, to merchandise the souls of men (Revelation 18:11-13).

Are you familiar with any churches and international entities with this reverberation?

We are now in the Last Days of Babylon. The Lord Jesus Christ shall avenge his apostles and prophets on her (Revelation 18:20). However, the Whore is in complete denial that she is the Great Whore. Revelation 18:7-8 states: How much she hath glorified herself, and lived deliciously, so much torment and sorrow give her: for she saith in her heart, <u>I sit a queen,</u> and am no widow, and shall see no sorrow. Therefore shall her plagues come in one day, death, and mourning, and famine; and she shall be utterly burned with fire: for strong is the Lord God who judgeth her.

Ezekiel 16:15,24-25 But thou didst trust in thine own beauty, and playedst the harlot because of thy renown, and pouredst out thy fornication on every one that passed by; his it was. That thou hast built unto thee an eminent place, and hast made thee an high place in every street. Thou hast built thy high place at every head of the way, and hast made thy beauty to be abhorred, and hast opened thy feet to every one that passed by, and multiplied thy whoredoms.

Isaiah 4:1 And in that day seven women shall take hold of one man, saying, We will eat our own bread, and wear our own apparel: only let us be called by thy name, to take away our reproach.

These seven women represent the seven churches in the Book of Revelation, which represent the church today. There is a difference between the churches and the over-comers. The overcomers are those who have Come out of Babylon to go up to Zion.

Coming Up Hither

Jesus is calling His Bride - The Overcomers, to come up into the highest form of assembling, which is - Going onto Perfection. Revelation 4:1-2 states: After this I looked, and, behold, a door was opened in heaven: and the first voice which I heard was as it were of a trumpet talking with me; which said, Come up hither, and I will shew thee things which must be hereafter. And immediately I was in the spirit: and, behold, a throne was set in heaven, and one sat on the throne."

The realm of the throne of God is the Holy of Holies, the place of immortal perfection in the presence of God. Beginning with Revelation Chapter Four, we no longer see the word - Church, mentioned, only once in Revelation 22:16.

Coming up hither - is the next step once we have come out of Babylon. This is when we make the decision to go all the way with Jesus, leaving the religious systems behind to Go onto Perfection.

Hebrews 4:11 Let us labour therefore to enter his rest, lest any man fall after the same example of unbelief.

One Thing Is Needful

When Jesus showed up at the home of Martha and Mary in Luke 10:38-42, Mary sat at the feet of the Alpha and Omega to hear his word, while Martha was preoccupied with serving. Martha came to Jesus and said - Lord, don't you care that my sister has left me to serve alone? Bid her therefore that she help me. Jesus responded by saying: Martha, Martha, thou art careful and troubled about many things: But one thing is needful: and Mary hath chosen that good part, which shall not be taken away from her.

The following scriptures reveal the will of God to make Jesus our First Love (Revelation 2:4). Mary made Jesus her first love by being with Jesus. Martha was busy doing things for Jesus. The following scriptures from the Word of God, will help anchor your mind to Come out of Babylon (Doing and Going) and move into Zion (Being): Meeting Jesus Outside the Box:

Exodus 33:7a And Moses took the tabernacle, and pitched it without the camp, afar off from the camp, and called it the Tabernacle of the congregation.

Exodus 33:11b But his servant Joshua, the son of Nun, a young man, departed not out of the tabernacle.

Exodus 33:21 And the Lord said, Behold there is a place by me, and thou shalt stand upon a rock.

Hebrews 13:13 Let us go forth therefore unto him without the camp, bearing his reproach.

Deuteronomy 33:16b Let the blessing come upon the head of Joseph, and upon the top of the head of him that was separated from his brethren.

Psalm 91:1 He that dwelleth in the secret place of the most High shall abide under the shadow of the Almighty.

Isaiah 26:20 Come, my people, enter thou into thy chambers, and shut the door about thee: hide thyself as it were for a little moment, until the indignation be overpast.

Isaiah 32:18 My people shall dwell in a peaceable habitation, sure dwellings, and quiet resting places.

Come Away My Beloved (Read all of the Song of Solomon).

Jeremiah 3:14 I will take you one of a city, and two of a family and bring you unto Zion.

Matthew 6:33 Seek first the kingdom of God.

The kingdom of God is the Kings Domain. Jesus wants us dwelling in the throne of His presence.

Mark 3:14 He ordained the twelve disciples that they should be with him.

John 6:29 This is the work of God, that you believe on him whom he has sent.

John 8:31 If you abide in my word, then you are truly my disciples.

Galatians 1:10 For do I now persuade men, or God? Or do I seek to please men? For if I yet pleased men, I should not be a servant of Christ.

I Corinthians 1:9 We are called to fellowship with Jesus.

Galatians 1:15-17 But when it pleased God, who separated me from my mother's womb, and called me by his grace to reveal his son in me that I might preach him among the heathen; <u>immediately I considered not with flesh and blood</u>. Neither went I up to Jerusalem to them which were apostles before me; but I went into Arabia, and returned again unto Damascus.

Galatians 4:1-2 Now I say, That the heir, as long as he is a child, differeth nothing from a servant, though he be lord of all; But is under tutors and governors until the time appointed of the father.

This verse could be used to support the idea of going to church. However, if the church is not giving you the Milk of the Word, - which is the Doctrine of Christ (Hebrews 5:12-Hebrews 6:1-2), based in II John 8-11, we are to leave that church immediately.

Philippians 3:8 I count all things but loss for the excellency of the knowledge of if Christ Jesus my Lord: for whom I have suffered the loss of all things, and do but count them as dung, that I may win Christ.

II Thessalonians 2:14 He called you by our gospel, to the obtaining of the glory of our Lord Jesus Christ.

Hebrews 6:1 Let us go onto perfection.

Birds Flock Together - Eagles Soar Alone

In 1989, after twenty years of going to many types of churches, conventions and seminars, and attending three Bible schools for a time, I was walking out my front door on the way to church one Sunday morning when I felt the Lord say: "Enough is enough, Come out of Babylon." I went back in my apartment, changed into my shorts and T-shirt, and went golfing. I never felt so spiritually liberated, I never looked back, and never regretted it.

I live along the bluff-line of a river valley in North America. Every so often we are fortunate to see an eagle soaring through the valley. On occasion, there are two or three of them together, yet they each seem to soar independently. This experience is a nice analogy for us to begin touching the face of infinity - to spread wide the wings of our spirit, and soar high and hard on the winds of the never-ending expanse of the presence of the Lord Jesus Christ.

He has placed a few other spiritual eagles in my life, as He will do for you, so that you can be encouraged and encourage them. The Lord Jesus Christ is building His Temple = His Body, in the Earth, according to the counsel of His Holy Spirit, not the religious systems of man:

I Corinthians 12:13 For <u>by one Spirit</u> are we all baptized into one body.

Ephesians 2:19-22 Now therefore ye are no more strangers and foreigners, but fellow citizens with the saints, and of the household of God; And are built upon the foundation of apostles and prophets, Jesus Christ himself being the chief cornerstone; In whom all the building fitly framed together groweth unto an holy temple in the Lord: In whom ye also are builded together for an habitation of God <u>through the Spirit</u>.

When people ask you - Are you under authority? Respond by asking them - Do you mean under Levitical Authority (Babylon) or under the Order of Melchizedek (Zion) (Hebrews 7:11). This type of reciprocation will have their eyes blinking like a bullfrog in a Texas hailstorm. When they say - Don't you belong to a church? Tell them - We don't go to church, we are the Church - The Church of the Firstborn.

> Hebrews 12: 22-24 - But ye are come unto mount Zion, and unto the city of the living God, the heavenly Jerusalem, and to an innumerable company of angels, To the general assembly and church of the firstborn, which are written in heaven, and to God, the Judge of all, and to the spirits of just men made perfect, And to Jesus the mediator of the new covenant, and to the blood of sprinkling, that speaketh better things than that of Abel.

The last two verses of the Book of Acts, show us that the Apostle Paul had no association with the churches during the last stages of his life:

> And Paul dwelt two whole years in his own hired house, and received all that came in unto him, Preaching the kingdom of God, and teaching those things which concern the Lord Jesus Christ, with all confidence, no man forbidding him (Acts 28:30-31).

Paul came to the place in his relationship with Jesus, where he knew the true essence was to attain immortality - the resurrection of the dead. He told the church at Corinth: What advantageth it me if the dead rise not? Let us eat and drink; for tomorrow we die (I Corinthians 15:32).

The Pearl of Great Price

The kingdom of heaven is like unto a merchant man, seeking goodly pearls: who, when he had found one pearl of great price, went and sold all that he had and bought it (Matthew 13: 46).

When we discover that the ultimate intention of Jesus for our lives is to Go onto Perfection, sometimes our first inclination is to naturally gravitate back to the church we came out of, and tell them the truth. Based on my experience, they will not listen. This is why Jeremiah 15:19b states: Let them return unto thee; but return not thou unto them.

We would have healed Babylon, but she was not healed: forsake her, and let us go every one into his own country (Jeremiah 51:9).

Kisser's and Cleavers

In the Book of Ruth, we find an account which can be used as a figure of those who cleave to the message of Coming out of Babylon and Going onto Perfection, and those that merely kiss the message:

And they lifted up their voice, and wept again: and Orpah kissed her mother in law; but Ruth clave unto her (Ruth 1:14).

The Time is Now

Some will wonder - If we don't go to church, where will we worship the Lord?
Jesus told the woman at the well: Woman, believe me,

the hour cometh, when ye shall neither in this mountain, nor yet at Jerusalem, worship the Father. Ye worship ye know not what: we know what we worship: for salvation is of the Jews. <u>But the hour cometh,</u> <u>and now is</u>, when the true worshippers shall worship the Father in spirit and in truth: for the Father seeketh such to worship him. God is a spirit: and they that worship him must worship him in spirit and in truth (John 4:21-24).

To recap: The will of the Lord Jesus Christ for our lives is to come out of Babylon, so that we may come up hither into Zion – Going onto Perfection, laboring to enter the rest of God.

Available Light

Album: Presto

the restless wind
has seen all things
in every kind of light
rising with the full moon
to go howling through the night

the sleepless wind
has heard all things
between the sea and sky
in the canyons of the city
you can hear the buildings cry

oh the wind can carry
all the voices of the sea
oh the wind can carry
all the echoes home to me

Run with wind and weather
To the music of the sea
All four winds together
Can't bring the world to me
Chase the wind around the world
I want to look at life – In the available light

play of light
a photograph
the way I used to be
some half-forgotten stranger
doesn't mean that much to me

trick of light
moving picture
moments caught in flight
make the shadows darker
or the colors shine to bright

oh the light can carry
all the visions of the sea
oh the light can carry
all the images to me

Run to light from shadow
Sun gives me no rest
Promise offered in the east
Broken in the west
Chase the sun around the world
I want to look at life – In the available light

All four winds together
Can't bring the world to me
Shadows hide the play of light
So much I want to see
Chase the light around the world
I want to look at life – In the available light

I'll go with the wind
I'll stand in the light

CHAPTER TEN

The Second Ascension

Think of the inner life - where the music exists.
- Yo Yo Ma

W hen Adam and Eve fell in the Garden of Eden, they fell out of Immortality. They fell from being clothed in the crystal brilliance of the Glory of God from within themselves. Jesus Christ came to reverse the curse, to restore us back to the glory that Adam and Eve lost. Colossians 1:27 blazons this truth: Christ in you, the hope of glory.

The Second Man

The following seemingly simple three verses of glistening light - solidify the true nature of the Second Coming:

I Corinthians 15:45-47 And so it is written, The first man Adam was made a living soul; the last Adam was made a quickening spirit. Howbeit that was not first which is spiritual, but that which is natural; and afterward that which is spiritual. The first man is of the earth, earthy: <u>the second man is the Lord from heaven</u>.

Jesus Christ was born into Earth as the Son of Man – The First Man Adam. However, Jesus was the Last Adam - The Last First Man. We know he was the Last First Man - in that He became the Second Man. Ephesians 2:15-16 declares: Having abolished in his flesh the enmity (Adam), even the law of commandments contained in ordinances; <u>for to make in himself of twain one new man</u>, so making peace; And that he might reconcile both unto God in one body by the cross, having slain the enmity thereby.

After Jesus had slain the First Man Adam on the cross, He was resurrected as the Second Man who now is the Quickening Spirit. Hence, I Corinthians 15:46 says: "First the natural and afterward the spiritual." The First Man is natural - the Second Man is spiritual. Evidenced on this passage in First Corinthians, we see only two men on Earth. These same two men appear in Colossians 3:9-10: "Put off the old man, and put on the new man." Consequently, it is not irrational to conclude the following:

Adam = The Old Man = The First Man = A Living Soul.

Christ = The New Man = The Second Man the Lord from Heaven = A Quickening Spirit.

Considering the Overly-Literal Return of Jesus

You may wonder, Do you believe Jesus is literally coming back in His body? Yes. Jesus is literally coming back in His body -The Body of Christ, which is the fullness of Him (Ephesians 1:22-23). He is coming within us - Spirit, Soul, and Body. The way we know Jesus is through the Word of God (The Bible) and through the increase of His presence in us (The Holy Spirit). The New Testament is clear that the coming of the Lord is a progression of His presence within us.

Strange teachers and apostles (II Peter 2:1 and Revelation 2:2) are romancing us with the vision of Jesus thundering from the invisible realms to rapture the saints into the cumulus clouds - ruining the crease in our new white robes, as we dodge Lear Jets and 747s until taken to Heaven. For seven years we will wine and dine at the marriage supper of the Lamb, as fierce tribulation ensues, as the Anti-Christ is cracking the whip on the inhabitants of Earth.

Personally, when I was enmeshed within these strange contrivances, I questioned whether I really wanted to be Raptured - I would have felt like an escaping chicken. I preferred to hang around the planet exercising my faith to cast the Devil out of the Anti-Christ, then carry on with the business of saving as many as I could. I thought - Where is the love for humanity in wanting to be Raptured away?

Staying in tune with the overly-literal interpretation of the coming of the Lord, consider this:

We have been told the New Jerusalem is a literal city. This presupposes it will be obtrusively positioned in geographical Israel. For now, we will disregard that Revelation 3:12 says: "To him that overcometh I shall write upon him the name of the city of God, which is New Jerusalem." According to Revelation 21:16, the city is 12 furlongs high, deep, and wide. In the measurements of today, this city would be 1,500 miles high, deep, and wide. How would it be situated in natural Israel which is 90 miles east to west, and 120 miles north to south?

Tel Aviv would be crushed, along with everybody and everything else. Let's not think about that for now. Once the

181

New Jerusalem is on Earth, Jesus will be calling the shots from the Throne Room. Hopefully, He will clear His schedule so we can meet Him face to face, then climb on His lap and finally hear those golden words drip like honey into our ears - Well done, good and faithful servant.

According to Revelation 20:4b, Jesus will reign on Earth for a thousand years. Not wanting to appear obtuse to the overly-literal interpretation, we will estimate that one hundred million believers are waiting in line to see Jesus. Each of us will have 30 minutes with Him. There are 525,600 minutes in a year, divided by 30 minutes = 17,520 believers will see Jesus the first year. Will they be scheduling appointments? Who will wait that long? For one hundred million believers to each see Jesus for 30 minutes would take 5,707.76 years. Yet, He is only here for a thousand years. What's more, we have a situation - Revelation 7:9a tells us: And I saw a great multitude, which no man could number.

Another question is - Where will all the stables be set up for the untold millions of white horses we flew in on from heaven? (Revelation 19:14). All those that press for the literal interpretation, should put their money where there mouth is and become equestrians.

This is a dreadful interpretation of the spiritual book called the Bible. The Rapture teaching swoons you into complacency; - waiting around for Jesus, when we should be pursuing the increase of his presence within us through fasting, prayer, and meditation of His Word. Let's take a look at the true coming of the Lord - within us.

The remainder of this chapter will provide the spiritual interpretation of the coming of Jesus Christ, stripping away interpretive distortions and dogmas advanced from the unspiritual interpretations. Around 1990, while living in Dallas, Texas, my whole perspective of the coming of the Lord shifted when I read the following verse:

He shall come to be glorified in the saints, and to be admired in all them that believe (because our testimony among you was believed) in that day (II Thessalonians 1:10).

Jesus is Coming Within Us

Before we look at the scriptures used by many to support the idea that Jesus will soon be stepping out of the spiritual stratosphere to whisk us away into the sky, let's take a look at the scriptures that clearly indicate that we are to focus on Jesus coming in His Glory within us:

Luke 17:19 –24 And when he was demanded of the Pharisees, when the kingdom of God should come, he answered them and said, The kingdom of God cometh not with observation: Neither shall they say, Lo here! or, lo there! For, behold the kingdom of God is within you. (The Kingdom of God is within you because the King of Kings is within you). The days will come when you will desire to see one of the days of the Son of man, and shall not see it. (How true is that!!) And they shall say unto you, See here; or, see there: go not after them, nor follow them. For as the lightening, that lighteneth out of the one part under heaven, shineth unto the other part of heaven; so shall also the Son of man be in his day.

The Greek word for – Lightning, is astrape, which means, bright shining. Jesus references the Sun which shines from one part of the sky to the other. Jesus substantiates this thought in Matthew 24:27: "For as the lightening (bright shining) cometh out of the east and shineth even unto the west; so shall also the coming of the Son of man be." Keep in mind - Jesus is the Bright and Morning Star (Revelation 22:16).

Peter 1:19 Take heed, as unto a light that shineth in a dark place, until the day dawn and the daystar (Jesus) arise in your hearts.

Revelation 2:28 To him that overcomes, he shall inherit the morning star.

The Day of the Daystar = The Day of the Lord. There are only two days according to scripture: The Day of Adam, the first man, and the Day of the Lord, the second man (I Corinthians 15:45-47).

Hebrews 7:15-16 After Melchizedek there arises another priest after the power of an endless life.

John 14:18, 20 I will not leave you comfortless: I will come to you. At that day, (The day of the Lord) ye shall know that I am in my Father, and ye in me, and I in you.

We enter the Day of the Lord when Jesus begins to ascend within us. In Revelation 1:10 John says – "I was in the spirit on the Lord's day." John was not saying – *Hey, guess what, I was in the spirit on Sunday morning.* The day of the Lord is the realm of spiritual light we enter as the Daystar ascends within us.

Romans 8:11 He shall quicken your mortal body by the Spirit in you.

Romans 8:18 The sufferings of this present time are

not worth to be compared to the glory that shall be revealed in us.

II Corinthians 4:10-11 The life of Jesus shall be manifest in our mortal flesh.

Ephesians 1:18 That you may know what is the hope of his calling, and what the riches of the glory of his inheritance in the saints.

Ephesians 3:20 He is able to do exceedingly by the power that works in us.

Galatians 1:16 Paul was called that, Christ would be revealed in him.

Galatians 4:19 Christ is being formed in you.

Colossians 1:27 Christ in you the hope of glory. (It does not say - Christ outside of you the hope of glory)

I John 3:3-4 When he shall appear (By the Spirit) we shall be like him; for we shall see (with our spiritual eyes) him as he is. And <u>every man that hath this hope in him</u> purifieth himself, even as he is pure.

The Trinity

Wherefore henceforth know we no man after the flesh; yea, though we have known Christ after the flesh, yet now henceforth know we him no more (II Corinthians 5:16).

The way we know Jesus now is by His presence, the Holy Spirit. If you believe in the Trinity, you believe that God is One:

Jesus is the Father and the Father is Jesus: He that hath seen me hath seen the Father (John 14:9). I and the Father are one (John 10:30).

The Holy Spirit is Jesus and Jesus is the Holy Spirit: And I will pray the Father, and he shall give you another Comforter, that he may abide with you for ever; Even the Spirit of truth…I will not leave you comfortless: I will come to you (John 14:16-18). For I know that this shall turn to my salvation through your prayer, and the supply of the Spirit of Jesus Christ (Philippians 1:19). The Spirit of Jesus = The Holy Spirit, there is no other Spirit in the Trinity. Jesus became a Quickening Spirit (I Corinthians 15:45).

The Father is the Holy Spirit and the Holy Spirit is the Father: Christ was raised from the dead by the glory of the Father (Romans 6:4). The Spirit raised Jesus from the dead (Romans 8:11).

For there are three that bear record in heaven, the Father, the Word, and the Holy Ghost: AND THESE THREE ARE ONE (I John 5:7). Revelation 19:13 declares: The name of Jesus is - The Word of God.

Acts 1:9-11

And when he had spoken these things, while they beheld, he was taken up; and a cloud received him out their sight. And while they looked stedfastly toward heaven as he went up, behold, two men stood by them in white apparel; Which also said, <u>ye men of Galilee, why stand ye gazing up into heaven</u>? this same Jesus which is taken up from you into heaven, shall so come in like manner as ye have seen him go into heaven.

The men of Galilee were the Apostles whom Jesus spent three years with. Had they already forgotten everything He had spoken to them concerning His coming back as the Holy Spirit - The Comforter? (John 14:16-20).

To be well-versed, it is essential to interpret the Bible with the Bible. The last time anyone on the planet knew Jesus after the realm of physical sight, was at the first ascension. Now we know Him by the Spirit in His second ascension. The passage above asserts that Jesus shall come in like manner - the manner that He left in was ascension. The manner in which He is coming again, is also in ascension. Jesus is ascending in us. Malachi 4:2 declares: "The Sun of righteousness shall arise with healing in his wings." This is echoed in II Peter 1:19b "The Day Star shall arise in your hearts." Jesus is coming to be glorified in the saints (II Thessalonians 1:10).

Matthew 10:23 But when they persecute you in this city, flee ye into another: for verily I say unto you, <u>Ye shall not have gone over the cities of Israel, till the Son of man be come.</u>

Jesus told the disciples in Luke 24:49 And, behold, I send the promise of my Father upon you: but <u>tarry ye in the city of Jerusalem, until ye be endued with power from on high.</u>

The coming of the Holy Spirit within them - was the second coming of Jesus. His coming is the progression of

His presence within us - Spirit, Soul, and Body.

The Rapture
I Thessalonians 4: 13-18

Verses 13-15: But I would not have you ignorant, brethren, concerning them which are asleep, that ye sorrow not, even as others, which have no hope. For if we believe that Jesus died and rose again, even so them also which sleep in Jesus will God bring with him. For this we say unto you by the word of the Lord, that we which are alive and remain (remain alive in the Spirit) unto the coming of the Lord shall not prevent (precede) them which are asleep.

There are passages in the Bible revealing that physical death can be equated to sleeping (Mark 5:39, Luke 8:52, and John 11:11). Consequently, this passage is quoted sometimes at funerals. However, if we stay within the context of First Thessalonians - Paul, Silvanus, and Timothy qualify what they meant by sleep in verses 13 and 14 in the next chapter:

Therefore let us not sleep, as do others; but let us watch and be sober. For they that sleep sleep in the night; and they that be drunken are drunken in the night. But let us, who are of the day, be sober, putting on the breastplate of faith and love; and for an helmet, the hope of salvation (I Thessalonians 5:6-8).

The writers of First Thessalonians were not making reference to physical death. They were speaking of believers that were in the darkness of their carnal mind -sleeping, rather than being awake to the things of the Spirit. The same principle of those in the church that were not awake to the moving of the Spirit is found in Ephesians 5:14: Wherefore he saith, Awake thou that sleepeth, and arise from the dead, and Christ shall give thee light.

The Ascension - Descension Principle

Verse 16: For the Lord himself shall descend from heaven with a shout, with the voice of the archangel, with the trump of God: and the dead in Christ shall rise first:

The Kingdom of Heaven is within us because the King of Kings is within us. The <u>Lord shall descend</u> from the higher realm of the Spirit (Heaven) within us, into the lower realms of our earthly nature, the Soul. His ascension within us as the Daystar, is also a descension from the higher realms of the Spirit - The second man the Lord from heaven (I Corinthians 15:47), is descending in us. Keep in mind, this is the Spiritual Interpretation, "comparing spirituals with spirituals" (I Corinthians 2:13).

<u>With a shout,</u> can be interpreted through Joel 3:16 - For the Lord shall also roar out of Zion, and utter his voice from Jerusalem; and the heavens and the earth shall shake.

<u>The voice of the archangel,</u> is referencing Michael in Daniel 12:1-2 - And at that time shall Michael stand up, the great prince which standeth for the children of thy people. And many of them that sleepeth in the dust of the earth shall awake, some to everlasting life, and some to everlasting contempt (paraphrased).

In both instances, the word Everlasting, is the Hebrew word, Olam, which means - Time Unknown, not Endless. Michael means - One who is like God. Michael is the angelic person-ification of Jesus Christ = The New Man = The Second Man the Lord from Heaven, standing up within us, awakening us from our sleep in the dust of our earthly nature. All of this can be distilled down to the simple understanding of putting off the old man and putting on the new man (Ephesians 4:22-24).

The trump of God, is the last trump in I Corinthians 15:52 which decrees: "The dead shall be raised incorruptible and we shall be changed." The dead are the Dead in Christ that shall rise first. To understand what Dead in Christ means, go back to Chapter Seven and review the subtext: The Baptism into Death.

> **Verse 17:** Then we which are alive and remain, shall be caught up together with them in the clouds, to meet the Lord in the air: and so shall we ever be with the Lord.

The writers to those in Thessalonica, admitted that they were not yet - Dead in Christ. Paul said – "I die daily." When the Old Man (Death) is swallowed up by the New Man (Life), there is a death to Death, in those that have fully put on the New Man - that have grown up into the Perfect Man (Ephesians 4:13). These are they, that are caught up into the cloud of the Presence of God = The Baptism into the Cloud (I Corinthians 10:1-2). The word – Clouds, in verse 17, is the Greek word - Nephele, it actually means, cloudiness – it does not freely assume more than one cloud. At any rate, this interpretation is consistent with the Doctrine of Christ and the Pattern of our Spiritual Growth revealed to us in the Tabernacle of Moses.

The word – air, in verse 17 – "To meet the Lord in the air" means, we will be caught up in the Spirit – caught up into the presence of the Lord - here on Earth, in this natural atmosphere. We will no longer be subject to the prince of the power of <u>the air</u>, the spirit that now worketh in the children of disobedience (Ephesians 2:2). Rather, the glory of the Lord shall be manifest in the atmosphere. Should we really believe that we will be caught up into the clouds in the sky? then in those clouds, <u>remain ever with the Lord?</u>

Verse 18: Therefore comfort (exhort) one another with these words.

Matthew 24:48 says: "The evil servant said in his heart: My Lord delayeth his coming." Those that believe in the unspiritual interpretation of the Rapture, believe in their heart that the Lord is delaying His coming. II Peter 3:3-4 warns us: "Scoffers will say, Where is the promise of his coming?" Jesus said in Revelation 22:20 – "Surely, I come quickly." As we fast, pray, and meditate the word of God, Jesus shall ascend – descend quickly within us.

Ooops!

Another passage that is used by some to support the Unspiritual Interpretation of the Rapture is found in Matthew 22:1-14. Jesus spoke a parable of the Marriage Supper of the Lamb. In verses 11-14 it says:

And when the king came in to see the guests, he saw there a man which had not on a wedding garment: And he saith unto him, Friend, how camest thou in hither not having a wedding garment? And he was

191

speechless. Then said the king to the servants, Bind him hand and foot, and take him away, and cast him into outer darkness; there shall be weeping and gnashing of teeth. For many are called, but few are chosen.

Was this man accidentally Raptured?
No.
The Marriage Supper of the Lamb is when the Bride-groom (The Spirit) and the Bride (Our Soul) become one. It begins in the Holy Place at the Candlestick and the Table of Shewbread - the consummation actualizes in the Holy of Holies, the realm of intimate communion with the Lord.

This man the king called – Friend, was cast into the Outer Darkness, which represents the Outer Court of the Tabernacle of Moses. The Outer Court had no covering. It was subject to the natural light of the Sun. To be illuminated by the knowledge and wisdom of men, is darkness – Outer Darkness. The king had his servants take him to the place where he must start his spiritual growth: First, the Outer Court; Second, the Holy Place; and Lastly, the Holy of Holies.

There is no coming in sideways or coming through the back door with Jesus – it is never Your Way – it is always Yahweh.

Christ is Held in the Heavens Until the Restoration of All Things

For those who believe Jesus is coming back in view of our natural perception, take time to consider Acts 3: 20-21 -

And he shall send Jesus Christ, which before was preached unto you: Whom the heaven must receive until the times of restitution of all things, which God hath spoken by the mouth of all his holy prophets since the world (ages) began.

According to this passage, Jesus is not coming back UNTIL the restitution (restoration) of all things. What this means is: Jesus will be fully manifest in the Earth through mankind, when death is fully swallowed up of His life, in everyone. This is also known as the Dispensation of the Fullness of Times, when God shall gather together in one all things in Christ, both which are in heaven, and which are on earth; even in him (Ephesians 1:10). For other cross-references concerning this, please read: I Corinthians 15: 21-29 and Hebrews 2:8.

The Blessed Hope

Looking for that blessed hope, and the glorious appearing of the great God and Saviour Jesus Christ (Titus 2:13).

We can be waiting for a train to arrive - and be sleeping while we are waiting – and miss the train. However, if we are looking for the train, we will be awake. In order to be spiritually awake, and not miss the true coming of the Lord within us, we must fast, pray, and meditate upon the word of God. For more on this, read Chapter Sixteen - The Queen of the South.

The word – Appearing, is the Greek word - Epiphania, which means – to shine upon. Again, Jesus is the Daystar that is arising in our hearts (II Peter 1:19). " For it is God which worketh in you both to will and to do of his good pleasure" (Philippians 2:13).

Face to Face

For now we see through a glass darkly; but then face
to face: now I know in part, but then shall I know
even as also I am known (I Corinthians 13:12).

The Apostle Paul had no inclination of seeing Jesus face
to face in the natural world, but spiritually. Paul was the one
who wrote II Corinthians 5:16 "Wherefore henceforth know
we no man after the flesh: yea, though we have known
Christ after the flesh, yet now henceforth know we him no
more." Paul said, "I shall know even as I am known." He did
not say, "I shall see even as I am seen." We see Jesus face to
face as the eyes of our spiritual understanding are enlightened that we may know what is the hope of his calling, and
the riches of the glory of his inheritance <u>in the saints</u>
(Ephesians 1:18).

II Corinthians 4:6 heralds: For God, who commanded
the light to shine out of darkness, <u>hath</u> shined in our
hearts to give light of the knowledge of the glory of
God in the face of Jesus Christ.

If seeing Jesus in His glorified body face to face in the
natural world is what will transform us into our glorified
body, why were Peter, James, and John not immediately
transformed on the Mountain of Transfiguration when Jesus
was transfigured into His glorified body? (Matthew 17:1-
12) Instead, Peter morphed into a religious frame of mind in
verse 4 and said: "Lord, it is good for us to be here: if thou
wilt, let us make here three tabernacles; one for thee, and
one for Moses, and one for Elias."

Jesus is Coming in Clouds

Behold, he cometh with clouds and every eye shall
see him (Revelation 1:7).

We are seeing Him as the eyes of our spiritual understanding are being enlightened (Ephesians 1:18). Moses
endured by seeing him who is invisible (Hebrews 11:27).
Jesus said in John 5:19 "The Son can do nothing of himself,
but what he seeth the Father do." Jesus did not see the Father
with His natural eyes. Those waiting around for Jesus to
come into the natural world so they can see Him with their
natural eyes are those that, "are after the flesh do mind the
things of the flesh; but they that are after the spirit the things
of the spirit" (Romans 8:5-6). "The natural mind receives
not the things of the Spirit of God" (I Corinthians 2:14).

The Kingdom of God cometh not with observation
(Luke 17:20-23). Since the Kingdom of God is not coming
with observation, why would we think the King of Kings
will come with observation? The Kingdom is within us – it
is Christ in us, the hope of Glory (Colossians 1:27).

We shall behold the glory of His presence in and on us.
His presence will flood and saturate us as a cloud. We then
become the cloud He is appearing in. Jude 11-12 speaks of
those that went the way of Cain, and ran greedily after
Balaam, and perished in the gainsaying of Core – they were
called, clouds without water.

Alternately, we can become clouds with water - filled
with the rivers and fountains of living waters springing up
from our innermost being (John 7:38 and Jeremiah 2:13),
pouring out the former and latter rain (Joel 2:23 and Hosea
6:3).

195

Caiaphas Saw Jesus Coming in Clouds

Matthew 26:64 Jesus saith unto him, Thou hast said: nevertheless I say unto you, Hereafter shall ye see the Son of man sitting on the right hand of power, and coming in the clouds of heaven.

We are now seated with Jesus in heavenly places - (Ephesians 2:6). When this spiritual (existential) reality becomes manifest in the natural (experiential), then the world will see Jesus coming in the clouds of His presence through us. Jesus kept His promise to the Caiaphas – he and the other Temple Elite saw the reality of Jesus coming in the clouds of His Disciples, after the Day of Pentecost. Acts 4:6-7 states: And Annas the high priest and Caiaphas, and John, and Alexander, and as many as were of the kindred of the high priest, were gathered together at Jerusalem. And when they had set them in the midst, they asked, By what power, or by what name, have ye done this?

This occured after the Disciples were filled with the power of the Holy Spirit – through them, Jesus saved 5,000 men. Caiaphas, as Jesus promised him, saw the Alpha and Omega sitting on the right hand of power, and coming in the clouds of heaven – that the Disciples had become. With this in mind, we can understand the following verse.

The Sign of the Son of Man

Matthew 24:30-31 And then shall appear the sign of the Son of man in heaven: and then shall all the tribes of the earth mourn, and they shall see the Son of man coming in the clouds of heaven with power and great glory. And he shall send his angels (messangers) with a great sound of a trumpet, and they shall gather together his elect from the four winds, from one end of heaven to the other.

The Sign of the Son of Man is the Order of Melchizedek – The Royal Priesthood of Jesus, in which He is glorified. We are the angels (messengers) sounding the trumpet of the Word of God unto the four winds – throughout the earth. We shall be glorified with Jesus as He is revealed in us (Romans 8:17-18). Those in the Holy of Holies, who are living in the ascension consciousness of Jesus, will be so caught up in the presence of God, they will demonstrate the power and glory of the Lord, as Jesus did when He walked on Earth.

Jesus said in John 14:12-14 Verily, verily, I say unto you, He that believeth on me, the works that I do shall he do also; and greater works than these shall he do; because I go unto my Father. And whatsoever ye shall ask in my name, that will I do, that the Father my be glorified in the Son. If ye shall ask any thing in my name, I will do it.

Loving His Appearing

Henceforth there is laid up for me a crown of righteousness, which the Lord, the righteous judge, shall give me at that day: and not to me only, but unto all them also that love his appearing (II Timothy 4:8).

We can love the appearing of Jesus in us right now. Are you living in the Day of the Lord or The Day of Adam? The Day of the Lord = The Day of the New Man = The Day of the Second Man the Lord from Heaven = The Day of the Daystar, rising in our hearts.

As in the Days of Noah, so shall also the Coming of the Son of Man Be

Another passage that has been misconstrued concerning a rapture into the sky is Matthew 24:37-42. The portion that is used to affirm the catching away of the saints into the cumulus clouds are verses 40-42: Then shall two be in the field; the one shall be taken, and the other left. Two women shall be grinding at the mill; the one shall be taken, and the other left. Watch therefore: for ye know not what hour your Lord doth come.

By now it should be established that the Second Coming is the internal reality of the ascension of Jesus within us. In the passages above, the one taken represents the Old Man - the New Man is left. II Thessalonians 2:8 states: And then shall that Wicked be revealed, whom the Lord shall consume (Old Man is taken) with the spirit of his mouth, and shall destroy with the brightness of his coming (the New Man is left.

All scriptures should be interpreted with the rest of the Bible. The whole course of this chapter can be distilled down to the central theme of putting off the old man, and putting on the new man (Ephesians 4:22-24). We do this by fasting, prayer, and meditating the word of God.

Xanadu
Album: A Farewell to Kings

"To seek the sacred river Alph
To walk the caves of ice
To break my fast on honeydew
And drink the milk of Paradise...."

I had heard the whispered tales
Of immortality
The deepest mystery
From an ancient book. I took a clue
I scaled the frozen mountain tops
Of eastern lands unknown
Time and Man alone
Searching for the lost - Xanadu
Xanadu - To stand within the Pleasure Dome

Decreed by Kubla Khan
To taste anew the fruits of life
The last immortal man
To find the sacred river Alph
To walk the caves of ice
Oh, I will dine on honey dew
And drink the milk of Paradise

A thousand years have come and gone
But time has passed me by
Stars stopped in the sky
Frozen in an everlasting view
Waiting for the world to end
Weary of the night
Praying for the light
Prison of the lost - Xanadu

Xanadu - Held within the Pleasure Dome
Decreed by Kubla Kahn
To taste my bitter triumph
As a mad immortal man
Nevermore shall I return
Escape these caves of ice
for I have dined on honey dew
And drink the milk of Paradise

CHAPTER ELEVEN

Imagining Immortality

Being born is not a crime, so why must it carry
a death sentence?
- Robert Ettinger

During the Miss USA pageant in 1994, Miss Alabama was asked, If you could live forever, would you and why? Her answer was, I would not live forever, because we should not live forever, because if we were supposed to live forever, then we would live forever, but we cannot live forever, which is why I would not live forever.

Oh dear...

Thy will be done on earth, as it is in heaven

The word - Gospel, means Good News. Good News to a mortal is – You do not have to be mortal anymore.

Some may not share this sensibility – once they move beyond the simplicity of it, it gets complicated.

Jesus told us: When we pray, believe that the will of God would be done on earth as it is in heaven (Matthew 6:10). Within the traditional concept of Heaven, we imagine no death or mortality exists there. Consequently, it is the will of God that no death or mortality exists on Earth. Jesus came to destroy sin and death. Immortality is just beyond the furthest reaches of mortal imaginations, therefore, we need to renew our minds (Romans 12:2). I like the line spoken by Andy in the movie, *Shawshank Redemption*: I guess it all comes down to this - Get busy living, or get busy dying.

In the context of scripture, it is irrational to render immortality impossible. This places a limit on our spiritual growth, as well as placing a limit on the limitlessness of God, with whom all things are possible (Mark 10:27). Immortality begins in the threshold of our imagination. II Corinthians 10:5 says: "Cast down imaginations, and every high thing that exalteth itself against the knowledge of God, and bring every thought into the obedience of Christ." Negative thoughts which stem from death, are like birds – we can't stop them from flying over our head, but we can keep them from setting up a nest in our hair.

A majestic revelation is announced in I Corinthians 2:16 proclaiming: "We have the mind of Christ." The question is: Is the mind of Christ a mortal or immortal mind? The mind of Christ is immortal by virtue of Him being the King Immortal (I Timothy 1:17).

Let there be no misunderstanding, when the Word of God speaks of Immortality, it is not making a vague and extraneous reference of creating an immortal legacy for ourselves – that when a person dies, they live in the hearts and minds of those that knew them. This is the mortal definition of immortality. The Scriptural or Immortal definition of immortality is never dying - Spirit, Soul, and Body. No more funerals. This is the Life of the Ages that Jesus Christ has bestowed on us.

Woody Allen said, "I don't want to achieve immortality through my work – I want to achieve it through not dying." Come on Woody – Prophesy! The Bible discloses the reason some individuals entertain doubts of Immortality – They have "made a covenant with death and hell" (Isaiah 28:14-15). The Norton Introduction to Literature, states it this way: "The shorter the expectation of life, the more sluggish the mental processes. They seem hypnotized by the approach of death, so resigned to their fate, they do nothing to avoid it."

Mortality is Mainstream

In Shakespeare's play *Hamlet*, his mother seeks to console him after his Fathers murder at the hands of his uncle:

Gertrude: Thou know'st tis common—all that lives must die, passing through nature to eternity.
Hamlet: Ay, madam, it is common.

As some people get older, they actually begin romanticizing the misery of mortality. Jesus said: "Wide is the gate that leads to destruction and many are they that go therein, narrow is the path that leads to life, and few there be that find it" (Matthew 7:13-14).

Since Jesus Christ is the Resurrection, and we are the Body of Christ, the natural extrapolation is – We are the Body of the Resurrection - the Body of the King Immortal. Certainly the King Immortal desires to dwell in an Immortal temple. So then, how do we obtain our spiritual inheritance of Immortality? The answer is: Like everything else we receive from God - By Faith - believing that we <u>have</u> <u>received</u> what we are praying for (Mark 11:23-24). However, we must first renew our minds to the will of God in this area.

According to Romans 8:2 - The law of God = The law of the spirit of life in Christ Jesus, which has made us free from the law of sin and death. However, if we do not enact this law, by sowing to the spirit that we might live, then we are sowing to the flesh and we will physically die (Romans 8:13). The First Man = The Old Man - brought death into the Earth. The fall of Adam and Eve was a falling out of the immortal presence of God. Jesus Christ, as the New Man = The Second Man the Lord from heaven (I Corinthians 15:47), is coming within us to restore us back to Eden = Paradise = The Immortal Presence of God. Jesus said: I have come that you might have life, and have it more abundantly (John 10:10).

Immortal Oracles

Let him who speaks, speak the oracles of God (I Peter 4:11).

Jesus said: He that believeth on me, as the scripture hath said, out of his belly shall flow rivers of living water (John 7:38). These resilient springs that flow up out of the ocean of our spirit, remind us that our true identity is Immortal. The barrier separating us from moving into our true spiritual inheritance is in the conscious mind. Romans 12:2 decrees: "Be ye transformed by the renewing of your mind." The following are various Oracles of Immortality – let the Holy Spirit, the Grand Thought Adjuster, conform your mind to the Mind of Christ. It is time to leave behind the illusions of death, and begin drinking deeply from the living waters of the royal golden chalice - held to our lips by the hands of Jesus:

Psalm 102:19-20 For he hath looked down from the

height of his sanctuary; from heaven did the Lord behold the earth; to hear the groaning of the prisoner; to loose those that are appointed to death.

Isaiah 25:8 He will swallow up death in victory; and the Lord God shall wipe away the tears from off all faces.

John 6:48-50 I am the bread of life. Your fathers did eat manna in the wilderness, and <u>are</u> <u>dead</u>. This is the bread which cometh down from heaven, that a man may eat thereof, and not die.

Jesus was not talking about merely avoiding spiritual death. So he drew a clear distinction by reminding His listeners that their fathers are dead. Physically dead.
So we do not miss it - Jesus says it again…

John 6:58 This is the bread which came down from heaven: not as your fathers did eat manna, and <u>are</u> <u>dead</u>: he that eateth of this bread shall live for ever.

John 8:51 Verily, verily, I say unto you, If a man keep my saying, he shall never see death.

Romans 2:7 Seek for glory, honor, and immortality, the life of the ages.

Romans 8:11 The spirit that raised Jesus from the dead shall also quicken your mortal body.

I Corinthians 15:51 Behold, I shew you a mystery; We shall not all sleep, but we shall all be changed.

This passage is not speaking about babies sleeping in a

nursery, that need to have their diapers changed. Rather, it reveals the reality that exists for us to escape death, by being clothed in the glory of God.

I Corinthians 15:53 For this corruptible must put on incorruption, and this mortal must put on immortality.

Just as Jesus said in John 3:7 – "Ye must be born-again." He also inspired the pen of the Apostle Paul to inscript: "This mortal must put on immortality." If not, you will die. Putting on immortality is the same as putting on the new man (Colossians 3:10.

II Corinthians 3:18 We are changed into the same image from glory to glory, even by the Spirit of the Lord.

II Corinthians 4:11 The life of Jesus shall be manifest in your mortal flesh.

II Corinthians 5:4 For we that are in this tabernacle do groan, being burdened: not for that we would be unclothed (die physically), but clothed upon, that mortality might be swallowed up of life.

Philippians 3:10-11 That I may know him and the power of the resurrection, and the fellowship of his sufferings, being made conformable to his death; if by any means I might attain to the resurrection of the dead.

Philippians 3:20-21 For our conversation is in heaven; from whence we look for the Saviour, the Lord Jesus Christ: Who shall change our vile body, that it may be fashioned like unto his glorious body, according to the working whereby he is able to subdue all things unto himself.

II Thessalonians 5:23 The very God of peace sanctify you wholly that your whole spirit and soul and body be preserved blameless unto the coming of our Lord Jesus Christ.

II Timothy 1:9-10 The purpose of God is now manifested by the appearing of our Saviour, who has abolished death and has brought life and immortality to light through the gospel.

Hebrews 7:15-16 And it is yet far more evident: for that after the similitude of Melchizedek there ariseth another priest, Who is made, not after the law of carnal commandment, but after the power of an endless life.

Revelation 21:4 And God shall wipe away all tears from their eyes, and there shall be no more death, neither sorrow, nor crying, neither shall there be any more pain: for the former things are passed away.

Mortal Minded Martha

In John 11:25-28 when Jesus visited the home of Mary and Martha in Bethany, to comfort them after the death of their brother Lazarus, Jesus said to Martha:

I am the resurrection, and the life: he that believeth **in** me, though he were dead, yet shall he live: And whosoever liveth and believeth **in** me shall never die. Believest thou this? She saith unto him, Yea, Lord: I believe that thou art the Christ, the Son of God, which should come **into** the world. And when she had so said, she went her way, and called Mary her sister secretly, saying, The Master is come, and calleth for thee.

I have highlighted the two times Jesus used the word – in. The Greek word used is – eis, which means – into. Where the word – into, is translated properly, the Greek word is also – eis. We understand from Chapter Seven, that we believe <u>into</u> Jesus, as we pass from the Outer Court, through the Holy Place, and into the Holy of Holies – the realm of Immortality. Ephesians 4:15 says: "But speaking the truth in love, may grow up into (eis) him in all things, which is the head, even Christ." Our spiritual growth is a progression into the timeless and deathless presence of Jesus Christ.

Martha was locked into the lower levels of mortal consciousness. However, Jesus who has the keys of death and hell (Revelation 1:18), came to unlock her mortal mind by telling her she does not have to die, then asks her - Believest thou this?

The comfortable religious ideology of Martha was beginning to collapse. Not ready for the whirl - she endeavors to neutralize the question of the King of Kings regarding breaking her appointment with death, by merely acknowledging that He was the Son of God – she avoided the question. John 11:28 then states – "She went her way." The atmosphere was becoming infinite in a hurry, on her last nerve, she secretly slips over to Mary and said: Hey Mary, the Master was over there giving me a private symposium on Eternal Life Extension - maybe you should have a chat with him, He wants to free your mind.

Hearing the unfiltered word of God is sometimes like walking out of a movie theatre on a sunny afternoon, your eyes need time to adjust. Likewise, our consciousness needs time to adjust from mortal imaginations into immortal imaginations. Romans 10:17 states: "So then faith cometh by hearing, and hearing by the word of God." One preacher has said, "So faith comes by hearing and hearing and hearing and hearing..."

Cancel Your Appointment With Death

Many have used Hebrews 9:28 to serenade us into the grave. The mortal axiom – "Death is just a part of life" - has no foundation in the word of God. It's a lie. Death is not a part of Life, death is the end-result of living in the existence of mortal consciousness. Those that use this scripture to this end, usually never read the next verse:

Verse 28: And it is appointed unto men <u>once</u> to die, but after this the judgment.

Here comes the judgment...

Verse 29: <u>So Christ was once offered</u> to bear the sins of many; and unto them that look for him shall he appear the second time (within us) without sin unto salvation.

Keep in mind Psalm 102:20 - God wants to loose those that are appointed to death. As stated in the first portion of this chapter, it was Adam that appointed us to death. So Jesus came as the Last Adam in our place to destroy sin and death on the cross, opening the passage into the Holy of Holies of the presence of God to overcome sin and death - spirit, soul, and body. However, we must be <u>looking for Him</u> by sowing to the spirit. As we fast, pray, worship, and meditate the word,

His presence shall increasingly appear within us as the sun rising from glory to glory. II Peter 1:19 says: Take heed, as unto a light that shineth in a dark place until the day dawn (The Day of the Lord) and the daystar (Jesus) shall arise in our hearts.

The High Calling

The entire third chapter of The Epistle to the Philippians is a discourse of the spiritual quest of the Apostle Paul to obtain immortality, or, the Resurrection of the Dead. This is the fifth element in the Doctrine of Christ (Hebrews 6:2). Exhibited below, are the essential passages from this chapter which maintain this thought:

Verses 10-11: That I may know him, and the power of his resurrection, and the fellowship of his sufferings, being made conformable to his death; If by any means I might attain unto the resurrection of the dead.

Paul said in Romans 7:24 "Who shall deliver me from the body of this death?" Yes, Paul was born-again, his spirit was saved. However, salvation is a three-fold process: our spirit, soul, and body (I Thessalonians 5:23).

Verses 14-15: I press toward the mark for the prize of the high calling of God in Christ Jesus. Let us therefore, as many as be perfect, be thus minded: and if in any thing ye be otherwise minded, God shall reveal even this unto you.

The High Calling of God in Christ Jesus, is not laying around on the sofa being washed over by Christian Television while waiting to be Raptured. Neither is it waiting to physically die and go to heaven after your spirit has been born-again. Amos 6:1 declares: Woe to them that are at ease in Zion.

What need would exist to press toward the mark for the prize? We are to labour to enter the rest (Hebrews 4:11). Our spiritual journey in Jesus begins in the Outer Court, through the Holy Place, and into the Holy of Holies - the Realm of Life. In essence, Paul says in verse 15: If you guys are not going to believe me, God is going to have to reveal this truth to you.

> Verses 20-21: For our conversation (Citizenship) is in heaven; from whence also we look for the Saviour, the Lord Jesus Christ: Who shall change our vile body, that it may be fashioned like unto his glorious body, according to the working whereby he is able even to subdue all things unto himself.

There are three heavens - three dimensions of spiritual adventure: The Outer Court, The Holy Place, and the Holy of Holies. Ephesians 2:6 states: (God) "Hath raised us up together, and made us sit together in heavenly places in Christ Jesus." The question is: are we in the First Heaven, the Second Heaven, or the Third Heaven. The Holy of Holies is the Third Heaven - The Immortal Zone; that place in the presence of God, where there is - No More Death (Revelation 21:4).

In the preceding chapter, Paul writes: "For it is God which worketh in you both to will and to do of his good pleasure" (Philippians 2:13). The will of God and His good pleasure, is for Jesus Christ to be fully glorified in us – Spirit, Soul, and Body.

> The last enemy that shall be destroyed is death (I Corinthians 15:26).

To be Absent from the Body is to be Present with the Lord

The title of this subtext is found in II Corinthians 5:8. This passage of scripture is widely taken out of its context to support the notion that physical death is preferable to life on Earth. Verse 4 of this same chapter makes it clear by announcing: For we that are in this tabernacle do groan, being burdened: not for that we would be unclothed (physically die), but clothed upon, that mortality might be swallowed up of life.

II Corinthians 5: 6-8: Therefore we are always confident, knowing that, whilst we are at home in the body, we are absent from the Lord: For we walk by faith, not by sight: We are confident, I say, and willing rather to be absent from the body, and to be present with the Lord.

If we are minding the things of the flesh, instead of the things of the spirit (Romans 8:5), then we are not walking by faith, but by sight – we are at home in the body (The Flesh), and absent from the Lord (The Spirit). II Corinthians 3:17-18 says: Now the Lord is that Spirit: and where the Spirit of the Lord is, there is liberty. But we all, with open face, beholding as in a glass the glory of the Lord, are changed in to same image from glory to glory, even as by the Spirit of the Lord.

II Corinthians 5: 9-10 Wherefore we labour, that, whether present or absent, we may be accepted of him. For we must all appear before the judgment seat of Christ; that every one may receive the things done in his body, according to that he hath done, whether it be good or bad.

There is no retroactive interference in my mind to boldly announce that we all appear before the judgment seat of Christ every hour of the day. Jesus said: And this is the condemnation (judgment), that light (life) is come into the world, and men loved darkness (death) rather than light, because their deeds were evil (John 3:19).

The Judgment of God is the Law of Cause and Effect - found in Galatians 6:7-8: Be not deceived; God is not mocked: for <u>whatsoever</u> a man soweth, that shall he also reap. For he that soweth to his flesh shall of the flesh reap corruption; but he that soweth to the Spirit shall of the Spirit reap life everlasting (The Life of the Ages).

Question: What is the meaning of life?
Answer: To be around to answer the question.

Witch Hunt
Album: Moving Pictures

The night is black
Without a moon
The air is thick, and still

The vigilantes gather on
The lonely torchlit hill

Features distorted in the flickering light
The faces are twisted and grotesque
Silent and stern in the sweltering night
The mob moves likes demons possessed
Quiet in conscience, calm in their right
Confident their ways are best

The righteous rise
With burning eyes
Of hatred and ill-will

Madmen fed on fear and lies
To beat, and burn, and kill

They say there are strangers, who threaten us
In our immigrants and infidels
They say there is strangeness, too dangerous
In our theatres and bookstore shelves
Those who know what's best for us –
Must rise and save us from ourselves

Quick to judge
Quick to anger
Slow to understand

Ignorance and prejudice
And fear
Walk hand in hand

CHAPTER TWELVE

Hell: The Cruel Illusion

Religion says: You might be going to Hell. Spirituality
says: We are coming out of Hell.
- Unknown

When I was a kid, I had to ride my old Schwinn bicy-
cle by the graveyard in my hometown each day on
my paper route. I would get the willies fearing for the dead
who were suffering in the swirling orange flames of Hell.
When evening came, especially at dark, I would do everything I could to avoid riding past the black metal fence
which surrounded the eerie calm.

I imagined the silent screams of the dead - wondering
how many of the people buried beneath the slow sway of the
towering oaks and evergreens, would ever have any hope.
Why was there a fence? Who would want to go in there? Or
worse – who were they trying to keep from coming out! In
my young mind, the graveyard was like the throne of the
Devil, and all the cynical black demons were flying around
in there, waiting for us.

For a young inducible mind – this was a living night-mare.

Who could you talk to about your fear of Hell? - every-one believed in it. I could not run to the sanctuary of the loving arms of my Mom, she also believed in Hell. I was trapped with no way out. My childhood was typical of anyone that grew up in a mainline church in North America. You were handed a simple package: If you believe in God and go to church, you go to Heaven, if not, you are going to Hell…for Eternity. Even though I believed in God, and went to Church and SundaySchool, I always thought -Why should I deserve to go to Heaven? simply because I attend Church - how could I really love and trust God, if I knew He was sending people to Hell?

A Gallop poll taken in 1993 - found that sixty percent of Americans believe in Hell, four percent thought they would end up there after death. The religious systems around the world have hundreds of millions of people checkmated with false fear. The leadership has not done their homework, or - they need to follow the company line and not upset the applecart.

For this planet-wide system that calls itself the Church, losing control on the international village - would result in the loss of billions of dollars on an annual basis. Chances are, many would prefer that their attendees would not ques-tion their authority – or their lack of authority. Within the fifteenth chapter of II Samuel, it records how Absalom stole the hearts of the men of Israel away from his father David, and they went in their simplicity, and they knew not anything. How prophetically correct Jesus was, when he spoke of wolves in sheep's clothing.

The Origination of the word Hell

Within the pantheon of Scandinavian mythology there exists the Norse goddess of death, who rules the bleak underworld of Niflheim – her name is Hel. She is the daughter of Loki the trickster, and his wife Angurboda. Souls that did not respond to the celestial solicitations of the Norse Gods were considered enemies. Consequently, they were not allowed to ascend to Valhalla, the palace of Odin, but were boiled alive in the cauldron Hvengelmir.

As a result of this mythology, when the Vikings were on their quest to conquer the world in the eighth and ninth century, their mythology was integrated into church theology. Subsequently, the word Hell was placed on the Hebrew word Sheol, which is the Old Testament equivalent of the Greek word Hades in the New Testament, which has been translated to Hell. Two other Greek words in the New Testament, Gehenna and Tartarus, have also been translated to Hell in most of the popular translations of the Bible.

The mythological doctrine of Eternal Hell Fire – is easy to throw into a tail-spin, shine the light on, and finally - evaporate. In the following sections of this chapter, we will look at every verse in the New Testament where the word Hell has been imposed, beginning with the Greek word, Gehenna.

The Smoking Gun

Gehenna is found in the original manuscripts of the New Testament twelve times. Gehenna was the local dump outside the south gate of the city of Jerusalem where all garbage was burned. In the Old Testament, it is known as The Valley of Hinnom. Every time the term Hell Fire is used in the New Testament, Gehenna is what Jesus was referring to.

If we are going to believe in the Literal Interpretation of

Hell Fire = Gehenna Fire – we find ourselves in a downward spiral. This fixation forces us to embrace the assumption that there is now - billions of men, women, and their children, endlessly writhing within intense seething flames just south of modern day Jerusalem. This notion would not bolster confidence within the tourism industry in Israel. Envision the enormous display of pillars of smoke billowing into the atmosphere, causing the cancellations of flights in the surrounding regions and around our blue planet forever. This concept certainly causes us to be less optimistic that God is a good environmentalist.

In Jeremiah 7:30-31 the Lord reprimands the children of Judah for doing evil abominations in his sight – they were burning their sons and daughters in the Valley of Hinnom, which God said: I commanded them not, neither came it into my heart.

In Luke 9:52-56 James and John asked Jesus if they should call fire down from heaven and consume Samaria for not receiving Jesus into their city. Jesus turned and rebuked them, and said - Ye know not what spirit you are of. For the Son of man is not come to destroy men's lives, but to save them.

In the same way, those that preach the satanic blasphemy of God punishing people in endless Hell-Fire - know not what spirit they are of.

Let's look at the twelve times Gehenna is mentioned in the New Testament starting with the ninth chapter of Mark, the most descriptive passage on Gehenna:

> Mark 9:43-50 And if thine hand offend thee, cut it off: it is better for thee to enter into life maimed, than having two hands to go into hell (Gehenna) into the fire that never shall be quenched: Where their worm dieth not, and the fire is not quenched. And if thy foot offend thee, cut it off: it is better for thee to

enter halt into life, than having two feet to be cast into hell (Gehenna) into the fire that never shall be quenched: Where their worm dieth not, and the fire is not quenched. And if thine eye offend thee, pluck it out: it is better for thee to enter into the kingdom of God with one eye, than having two eyes to be cast into hell (Gehenna) fire: Where their worm dieth not, and the fire is not quenched. <u>For every one shall be salted with fire</u>, and every sacrifice shall be salted with salt. Salt is good: but if the salt have lost his saltness, wherewith will ye season it? Have salt in yourselves, and have peace one with another.

Jesus was not condoning self-mutilation, He was speaking hyperbolically to emphasize the impossibility of saving ourselves from the sinful nature of Adam within us. Because Jesus knew this was true – He cuts to the white heat of it in verse 49: "Everyone shall be salted with fire" - believers and non-believers alike. Isaiah 66:16 says: "For by fire and by sword shall the Lord plead with all flesh." In Luke 12:42-48 Jesus tells the parable of the unprofitable servant who will be appointed his portion with the unbelievers.

This fire is not literal fire – it is the fire of the presence of God burning out all mortal impurities within us. Isaiah 4:4 announces that God will cleanse the daughters of Zion and purge the blood of Jerusalem by the spirit of judgment and by the spirit of burning.

Where Their Worm Dieth Not

The fire that is not quenched in Mark 9 will be elaborated upon at the end of this chapter in the subtext Unquenchable Fire. For now, let's take a look at -Where their worm dieth not. The Young's Literal Translation of the

Bible says: <u>Where their worm is not dying, and the fire is not being quenched</u>. Staying in the context of Gehenna – the worms would feed off the refuse – likewise, the Holy Spirit will keep eating away at every vestige of mortal impurities within us until we are a Bride - "without spot or wrinkle, or any such thing" (Ephesians 5:27). The worm is not dying as long as it has some garbage to feed on. As long as we remain mortal - that little worm will keep chewing away at our mortality.

> Matthew 5:22 Whosoever, shall say, Thou fool, shall be in danger of hell (Gehenna) fire.

> Matthew 5:29 If the right eye offend thee, pluck it out, and cast it from thee: for it is profitable for thee that one of thy members should perish, and not that thy whole body should be cast into hell (Gehenna).

> Matthew 5:30 If thy right hand offend thee, cut it off, and cast it from thee: for it is profitable for thee that one of thy members should perish, and not that thy whole body should be cast into hell (Gehenna).

In the context of the last three verses, Jesus expresses the Sisyphean anguish of keeping the law to perfection and our inability to control the strength of the fleshly nature. It is only by the working of the Holy Spirit and the purging fire of His presence within us, that mortal impurities will be burned out. Cutting off any part of our body - will not cause us to stand holy before the Lord. Again, Isaiah 4:4 states: The Lord shall wash away the filth of the daughters of Zion, and shall purge the blood of Jerusalem with the spirit of judgment and by the spirit of burning.

Matthew 10:28 And fear not them which are able to

kill the body, but are not able to kill the soul: but rather fear him which is able to destroy both soul and body in hell (Gehenna).

This is understood through the Baptism of Fire and Baptism into Death explained in Chapter Six. We know from Mark 9:49 that everyone shall be salted with the fire of Gehenna - which is symbolic of the purging process of the Spirit of God.

Not wavering from the Doctrine of Christ and the Tabernacle of Moses, we know that the final destiny for our spiritual growth is to Go Onto Perfection - For this mortal to put on immortality. As this happens, our Soul and Body shall be transformed, our Adamic nature will be killed - the soulish nature of the Old Man shall die, as the New Man appears. In the same vein - our mortal body shall give way to our immortal body.

Revelation 12:11 And they overcame him by the blood of the Lamb, and by the word of their testimony; and they loved not their lives (Soul) unto the death.

Matthew 18:9 And if thine eye offend thee, pluck it out, and cast it from thee: it is better for thee to enter into life with one eye, rather than having two eyes to be cast into hell (Gehenna) fire.

The explanation of this verse is the same as the verses from Matthew chapter five.

Matthew 23:15 Woe unto you, scribes and Pharisees, hypocrites! For ye compass sea and land to make one proselyte, and when he is made, ye make him twofold more the child of hell (Gehenna) than yourselves.

Any convert of the scribes and Pharisees, would add their hypocrisy to his own. Hence, his purging process would be double.

Matthew 23:33 Ye serpents, ye generation of vipers, how can ye escape the damnation of hell (Gehenna).

The word <u>damnation</u> is a Latin word placed on the Greek word Krisis, which of course, translated into English is - Crisis. When we act as serpents and vipers against the truth of God, we will find ourselves in a crisis situation of His promise to purge us with spiritual fire. For our God is a consuming fire (Hebrews 12:29) - burning us from the inside out.

Luke 12:5 But I will forewarn you whom ye shall fear: Fear him, which after he hath killed hath power to cast into hell (Gehenna); yea, I say unto you, Fear him.

This verse is along the same lines of Matthew 10:28 – with a twist. After we have put on immortality, we will still have the impression of freewill. If we are inclined to move against the Word of God and the leading of the Holy Spirit, the Spirit will continue to purge within.

James 3:6 And the tongue is a fire, a world of iniquity: so is the tongue among our members, that it defileth the whole body, and <u>setteth on fire the course of nature</u>; and it is set on fire of hell (Gehenna).

Jesus said: Out of the abundance of the heart, the mouth speaks (Matthew 12:34). If we are speaking negative words based in fear, hate, and bitterness - through the fire of Cause and Effect (The Course of Nature), God will mirror reflect back to us a harvest of what we have sown with our words.

Tarturus

The Greek word Tarturus appears only once in the New Testament. In Greek mythology, Tarturus and the Elysian Fields were the two main regions of the underworld ruled by Hades. In Homer, Zeus speaks to the Greek Gods warning them of his fury if they were ever were tempted with rebellious impulses: "Let no god, let no goddess attempt to curb my will...or I shall sieze him and cast him down to Tarturus."

Why would Bible translators place the word Hell on Hades - a person, and Tarturus - a place? Perhaps they thought since Tarturus and Hades are both nouns, they might be able to sneak it by us. These are clearly two different words that have two entirely different meanings. Should we expect anything less from those that translate – Aionios, to - Eternal? Evidently not.

II Peter 2:4 God spared not the angels (messengers) that sinned, but cast them down to hell (Tarturus) and delivered them into chains of darkness, to be reserved unto judgment.

If there really was a "Hell" – technically, Tarturus is it. However, it is not a real place. Tarturus is a mythological region to illustrate the experience we find ourselves in, if we are not aligning ourselves with the word of God. The entire context of the second chapter of II Peter, is speaking of false teachers that are more concerned in merchandising the souls of men (Revelation 18:12-13) than speaking the oracles of God. Consequently, they will live in the judgment of the lower realms of the chains of darkness, rather than living in the fullness of the light of Mount Zion of the Lord Jesus.

The Siren Call: David and Jonah in Hell?

Psalm 16:10 For thou wilt not leave my soul in hell; neither wilt thou suffer thine Holy One to see corruption.

Psalm 139:8 If I ascend up to heaven, thou art there: if I make my bed in hell thou are there.

Jonah 2:2 I cried by reason of my affliction unto the Lord, and he heard me; out of the belly of hell cried I, and thou heardest my voice.

As a Christian who had been attending fundamental and evangelical, Word-based churches, seminars, conventions, and Bible schools - these verses caused me to begin seriously questioning my belief system. How could it be that David and Jonah, men of God who were still living on earth, state that they were in Hell?

From over ten years of studying this topic in the Bible, comparing spirituals with spiritual, I no longer believe that Hell is a location, but a condition – the condition of darkness within us. If the Kingdom of Heaven is within us by the light of the Lord, it is my assertion, that any part of our soul (mind, will, and emotions) that we have not submitted to the Lord, that is still unenlightened, is weighed down by the darkness, death and despair, of the kingdom of Hell.

Sheol=Hades

I have chosen not to list the sixty-five times that Sheol shows up in the Old Testament. I believe it is sufficient to reveal that Sheol is indeed the Old Testament equivalent to the Greek word Hades in the New Testament. The following scriptures will show that Sheol and Hades are synonymous:

A1. Hosea 13:14 I will ransom them from the power of the grave (sheol), I will redeem them from death: O death, I will be thy plagues; O grave, (sheol) I will be thy destruction: repentance shall be hid from mine eyes.

A2. I Corinthians 15:55 O death, where is thy sting? O grave, (hades) where is thy victory?

B1. Psalm 16:10 For thou wilt not leave my soul in hell (sheol); neither wilt thou suffer thine Holy One to see corruption.

B2. Acts 2:27 Because thou wilt not leave my soul in hell (hades); neither wilt thou suffer thine Holy One to see corruption.

Shades of Hades

The rest of this chapter will deal with the eleven passages in the New Testament where the Greek word for Hell - is Hades. Within Greek mythology, Hades is a brother of Zeus – he is also the Lord of Darkness. Hence, in the New Testament, Hades is not a location, rather, Hades is used as a personification of the man of darkness = The First Man Adam, that is unyielding to the Lord of Light = The Lord Jesus Christ = The Word of God.

Matthew 11:23 and Luke 10:15 are synonymous in that they say: And thou, Capernaum, which are exalted unto heaven, shalt be brought down to hell (Hades).

Jesus singled out Capernaum – it was His hometown (Matthew 9:1 and Mark 2:1). Jesus said mighty works had been done in Capernaum, the presence of God was manifest in the city in a powerful way - it was exalted to heaven. Yet, the city did not repent, so it fell under the same judgment as Chorazin and Bethsaida. The judgment was the glory of God leaving the city – it was brought down into spiritual darkness, down into the clenching fist of Hades. Subsequently, the city of Capernaum no longer exists in Israel.

The Gates of Hades Will Not Prevail

Matthew 16:13-19 records: When Jesus came into the coasts of Caesarea Philippi, he asked his disciples, saying, Whom do men say that I the Son of man am? And they said, Some say that thou art John the Baptist: some, Elias; and others, Jeremias, or one of the prophets. He saith unto them, But whom say ye that I am? And Simon Peter answered and said, Thou art the Christ, the son of the living God. And Jesus answered and said unto him, Blessed art thou, Simon Barjona: for flesh and blood hath not revealed it unto thee, but my Father which is in heaven. And I say also unto thee, That thou art Peter, and <u>upon this rock I will build my church: and the gates of hell (Hades) shall not prevail against it</u>. And I will give unto thee the keys of the kingdom of heaven: and whatsoever thou shalt bind on earth shall be bound in heaven: and whatsoever thou shalt loose on earth shall be loosed in heaven.

The rock that Jesus is building His Church on is not Peter, - The Rock is the revelation of the word of God that opens the eyes of our spiritual understanding (Ephesians

1:17-18) – just as the Father in heaven opened Peters eyes. We need serious help if Peter is The Rock. In Matthew 16: 21-23, Jesus said unto Peter – "Get thee behind me Satan: thou art an offense unto me: for thou savourest not the things that be of God, but those that be of men." Directly after Peter received a revelation from God, he then moves into his fleshly mind and rebukes Jesus for saying that he must suffer many things and be killed.

Back to the issue at hand - Why did Jesus tell His disciples, the gates of hell (Hades) would not prevail against them? Were not the disciples of Jesus already "saved" from Hell? Furthermore, what does it mean - "the gates (plural) of hell"? If the disciples were already saved from Hell, why would they have an interest in going back in? This leaves an inquiry: Were the disciples outside or inside - the gates of Hell?

It is my unwavering conviction that Hell = Hades, is mortal consciousness - the spiritual darkness within our Soul. Through the Keys of the Kingdom, which are the promises of God, we can prevail against the different levels of darkness (gates of Hell) within us - as we renew our minds to the immortal light of the word of God. To further substantiate that Hell is mortal consciousness, read on through the next subtext.

The Apostle Paul Mentions Hell Only Once

You would think if Eternal Hell-Fire posed such a grand threat to humanity, the Apostle Paul who wrote one-third of the New Testament, would have warned us of this horrific doom at least three or four times on every page. And yet, even the one time he did mention Hades = Hell, most of the Bible Translators covered it up.

Honestly - what in the world is going on here?

For crying out loud....

The reality that Hades = Hell, is Mortal Consciousness, is validated in I Corinthians 15:55. However, it is not found in most Bibles. The only Bible I have found, that gave an honest translation from the Greek (I'm sure there may be others) is Young's Literal Translation: Where, O death, thy sting? Where, O hades, thy victory?

King James Version: O death, where is thy sting? O, grave where is thy victory?

New American Standard Version: O Death, where is your victory? O Death, where is your sting?

Why didn't the professional Bible translators place the word Hell on the Greek word Hades in this passage, like they did every other time in the New Testament?

The answer is: They didn't know what the Hades is going on. Again, this verse is the one and only time Paul mentions Hades – in the context of this mortal putting on immortality (I Corinthians 15:51-57). As Jesus, who is the Resurrection and the Life ascends within our Soul, Death and Hades will be swallowed up in His resurrection victory, to ultimately be manifested in our body – if we are sowing to the Spirit of Life in Christ Jesus, through fasting, prayer, and meditating His word.

The carnal mind is death (Romans 8:6). If we keep operating in the carnal mind, instead of the spiritual mind, our soul will be in darkness = Hades = Hell.

Lazarus and the Rich Man

The most popular passage in the Bible that is exploited by those who preach eternal hell-fire, is the parable of

Lazarus and the Rich Man - where the Rich Man lifted up his eyes in Hades (Luke 16 23). Like a five-faceted diamond gently turning with ethereal radiance, this parable is the fifth of five parables:

The parable of the Lost Sheep (Luke 15:4-7)
The parable of the Lost Coin (Luke 15:8-10)
The parable of the Prodigal Son (Luke 15:11-32)
The parable of the Faithful Steward (Luke 16:1-13)
The parable of Lazarus and the Rich Man (Luke 16:19-31)

Luke 15:3 says: *And he spake this parable unto them.* Present within the audience of Jesus were politicians, sinners, His disciples, and the Scribes and Pharisees. Jesus did not want to leave anyone present at his narration out of the picture, so he directed the parable of Lazarus and the Rich Man specifically towards the self-righteous leaders of Israel, that were there deriding the Alpha and Omega.

The upshot of this parable is the dealing of God with the Gentiles (Lazarus) and natural Israel (The Rich Man). The best way to understand this parable is to interpret the Bible with the Bible. In this case, read all of the eleventh chapter of the book of Romans.

Verse 19: There was a certain rich man, which was clothed in purple and fine linen, and fared sumptuously every day.

Purple is the color of royalty. Fine linen was worn by the priests of Israel. Jesus immediately grabbed the attention of the Scribes and Pharisees - who started shaking in their sandals, interrupting their conversation on whether they were going to have red or white wine that evening with dinner at their annual budget meeting - before they retired to their warm beds, fitted with 300-count Egyptian cotton sheets.

Verse 20: And there was a certain beggar named Lazarus, which was laid at his gate, full of sores.

Lazarus is the Greek equivalent to the Hebrew name Elazar, which means - one whom God helps. Lazarus laid at the gate of the Rich Man hoping he would help him out.

Verse 21: And desiring to be fed with the crumbs which fell from the rich mans table: moreover the dogs came and licked his sores.

It is obvious the Rich Man did not set up a clinic, local food shelter, or low-cost housing, to care for the people living on the streets in his city. It says, Lazarus was full of sores (verse 20), which did not accumulate overnight, but over a period of time. Therefore, the Rich Man was consistently uncompassionate.

Verse 22: And it came to pass, that the beggar died, and was carried by the angels into Abrahams bosom: the rich man also died, and was buried.

There is no mention whether Lazarus or the Rich Man were believers or nonbelievers. If Abraham's Bosom is Heaven - what happened to Abel, Seth, Enoch, and Noah - who serve the Lord before Abraham was born? Jesus was symbolically (this is a Parable) making reference of the coming of the New Covenant, which is being saved by grace, and the end of the Old Covenant of works, which was administered by the Israeli Leadership.
We see this in that - the rich man died and was buried.

This is pure symbolism – are we to presume that Lazarus was not buried? – and was carried by winged creatures up into the sky? Just as Dorothy was carried by flying-monkeys to the castle of the Wicked Witch of the West?

> **Verse 23:** And in hell (Hades = Spiritual Darkness = Mortal Consciousness) he lift up his eyes, being in torments, and seeth Abraham afar off, and Lazarus in his bosom.

The Greek word for hell in this verse is Hades. Hades is the condition of darkness within us, whether we are living on earth or have died. Until the immortal light of Jesus ascends within us, we will continue to be in Hades. Lazarus being in Abraham's Bosom reveals the sovereignty of the salvation of God.

> Romans 9:18 states: Therefore hath he mercy on whom he will have mercy, and whom he will he hardeneth. John 1: 12-13 states: But as many as received him, to them gave he power to become the sons of God, even to them that believe on his name: Which were born, not of blood, nor of the will of flesh, nor of the will of man, but of God.

> **Verse 24:** And he cried and said, Father Abraham, have mercy on me, and send Lazarus, that he may dip the tip of his finger in water, and cool my tongue; for I am tormented in this flame.

If the account of Lazarus and the Rich Man is literal - with literal fire, then we know that those in Hell will be able to carry on a conversation with those in Heaven. And also, that a drop of water, will provide some relief. In all reality, the Rich Man was being tormented by the Spirit of God burning the mortal impurities out of his soul. "For our God is a consuming fire" (Hebrews 12:29).

Verse 25: But Abraham said, Son, remember that thou in thy lifetime receivedst thy good things, and likewise Lazarus evil things: but now he is comforted, and thou art tormented.

It's interesting that the Rich Man called Abraham –Father (verse 24), and Abraham responded by calling him –Son (verse 25). Abraham did not forget the Covenant that God made with the Rich Man, that, In thy seed (Abraham) shall all nations be blessed. However, the Rich Man had been living high off the hog on the laurels of his natural birthright, not caring for the poor. He was being tormented by the conviction of the Holy Spirit.

Verse 26: And beside all this, between us and you there is a great gulf fixed: so that they which would pass from hence to you cannot; neither can they pass to us, that would come from thence.

This parable was spoken during the Old Covenant - Jesus had not yet shed His blood for humanity. It was only after His resurrection that the unbridgeable chasm was crossed. Only Jesus Christ is the bridge between darkness and light - Jesus said, And I, if I be lifted up from earth, will draw all men unto me (John 12:32).

Verse 27-28: Then he said, I pray thee therefore, father, that thou wouldest send him to my fathers house. For I have five brethren; that they may testify unto them, lest they also come into this place of torment.

These two verses reaffirm that Jesus was speaking of the Rich Man as a symbol of the leadership of Israel. The wealthiest tribe of Israel was the tribe of Judah. We find in Genesis 35: 22-23 - that Judah was born of Jacob and Leah who had six sons: Reuben, Simeon, Levi, Judah, Issachar, and Zebulun. The Rich Man is symbolic of Judah.

Verse 29: Abraham saith unto him, <u>They</u> have Moses and the prophets; let them hear them.

It was the priests of Israel that had Moses (The Law) and the writings of the prophets. This verse validates again, that Jesus had a parabolic message for the Scribes and Pharisees.

Verse 30-31: And he said, Nay, father Abraham: but if one went unto them from the dead, they will repent. And he said unto him, If they hear not Moses and the prophets, neither will they be persuaded though one rose from the dead.

The reason they would not hear Moses and the prophets is because Romans 11:8 records - "God gave them the spirit of slumber, eyes that they should not see, and ears that they should not hear unto this day." Even with the resurrection of Jesus they cannot hear. It is only by the grace of God opening our eyes that we can be saved. Again, please read all of the eleventh chapter of the Book of Romans – what Jesus was alluding to in the parable of Lazarus and the Rich Man, will become overwhelmingly clear.

To summarize: If the parable of Lazarus and the Rich Man is literal, it does not support the ideology of Eternal Damnation. Romans 11:25-27 declares:

For I would not, brethren, that ye should be ignorant of this mystery, lest ye should be wise in your own conceits: that blindness in part is happened to Israel (the Rich Man), until the fullness of the Gentiles (Lazarus) be come in. And so all Israel shall be saved: as it is written, There shall come out of Sion the Deliverer, and shall turn away ungodliness from Jacob: For this is my covenant unto them, when I shall take away their sin.

The Other Seven Times Hades is in the Bible

Acts 2:27 Of King David it says: Thou wilt not leave my soul in hell (Hades = Sheol), neither wilt thou suffer thine Holy One to see corruption.

David did not die and go to hell, yet there were times when he was in spiritual darkness, and was confident that the Lord would restore him into the light of His presence. David also being a prophet (Acts 2:29-30) wrote that God would raise up Christ.

Acts 2:31 He seeing this before spake of the resurrection of Christ, that his soul was not left in hell (Hades), neither did his flesh see corruption.

When Was Jesus in Hell?

Many believe that after Jesus died, He spent three days in Hell suffering in agony for our sins. Others believe He was in Hell on a preaching mission, and to track and whack the Devil. Both of these beliefs are untrue. The hell (spiritual darkness) that the soul of Jesus experienced, was on the cross spilling his blood for the sin of humanity, and being separated from the Father of Lights. Watching Mel Gibson's movie - *The Passion of the Christ*, will help convince you of this truth.

> Mark 15:33-34 records: "And when the sixth hour (12 noon) was come, there was darkness over the whole land until the ninth hour. And at the ninth hour Jesus cried with a loud voice, saying, Eloi, Eloi, lama, sabach-thani? Which is, being interpreted, My God, My God, why hast thou forsaken me?" After this, according to John 19:30 Jesus said - "It is finished." His suffering was over – the debt for the sin of the world was paid.

After Jesus died, He went to paradise. He told the man on the cross next to him in Luke 23:43: "Verily I say unto thee, Today shalt thou be with me in paradise." To further prove Jesus was in paradise with the Father, Luke 23:46 says, "And when Jesus had cried with a loud voice, he said, Father, into thy hands I commend my spirit: and having said thus, he gave up the ghost." After Jesus was resurrected on the third day, He then proceeded in the business of preaching...

> I Peter 3:18-20: For Christ also hath once suffered for sins, the just for the unjust, that he might bring us to God, being put to death in the flesh, <u>but quickened by the Spirit: By</u> which also he went and preached unto the spirits in prison; Which sometime were disobedient, when once the longsuffering of God waited in the days of Noah, while the ark was a preparing, wherein few, that is eight souls were saved by water.

It was after Jesus was resurrected - quickened by the Spirit, that He preached to those that had died. The proof that He was the Saviour of the world came from His resurrection.

Romans 4:25 states: Who was delivered for our offences, and was raised again for our justification.

I Peter 4:6 For this cause was the gospel preached also to them that are dead, that they might be judged according to men in the flesh, but live according to God in the spirit.

The holy oracle above is evidence that Jesus will save unbelievers after they physically die – this is yet another adjudication in assisting us in our apprehension of The Restoration of All Things – the fulfillment of the Abrahamic Covenant.

Hades in the Book of Revelation

Revelation 1:18 I am he that liveth, and was dead; and, behold, I am alive for evermore, Amen; and have the keys of death and hell (Hades).

We are to cease the keys of death and hell - to unlock the gates of darkness within us. Paradoxically, these keys are the Keys of the Kingdom, which Jesus referred to in Matthew 16:19. The keys to the gates of the perpetual increase of the presence of God - are the promises of God.

II Peter 1:3-4 broadcasts: According as his divine power hath given unto us all things that pertain to life and godliness, through the knowledge of him that hath called us to glory and virtue: Whereby are given unto us exceeding great and precious promises: that by these ye might be partakers of the divine nature, (moving from our humanity into our divinity) having escaped the corruption that is in the world through lust.

Revelation 6:8a And I looked, and behold a pale horse: and his name that sat on him was Death, and Hell (Hades) followed him.

This is the fourth seal of the Seven Seals in the Book of Revelation. This verse will be explained in my next book - *The Metaphorical Oracle: Understanding the Symbols in the Book of Revelation.*

The Lake of Fire

Revelation 20:13-14: And the sea gave up the dead which were in it; and death and hell delivered up the dead which were in them: and they were judged every man according to their works. And death and hell were cast into the lake of fire. This is the second death.

The dead in this passage refers to those that live in the carnal mind - which is death (Romans 8:6). Consequently, they have dead works - living in the flesh, not pursuing the presence of God. Many have believed that Hell is the Lake of Fire, yet it says - Death and Hell were cast into the Lake of Fire.

The lake of fire is simply symbolic of the purging process of the Holy Spirit – burning out all the mortal tarnish within us. The first man brought us into the First Death. The second man burns out the First Death, through the Second Death. The death of Death. Once this is complete, there shall be no more death – no more first or second death.

I like interpretations that you can't deny. You might not

agree with it, however - it's true anyway. Death is the last enemy that shall be destroyed (I Corinthians 15:26).

Unquenchable Fire

In Jeremiah 17: 27 - God warns Jerusalem that He would kindle a fire that would not be quenched, if they did not hallow the Sabbath day. We see this prophecy fulfilled in Jeremiah 52:13 - the fire was not quenched - it burned all the houses of Jerusalem. Yet, it is not burning today. Unquenchable Fire does not equate to Eternal fire.

By definition, Unquenchable merely means - Unextinguishable. For instance, a house may be roaring in flames so hot and thick, that fire-fighters would not be able to quench it. Yet, once the fire has burned the house to the ground, and has nothing left to feed on, it will go out. This is also the way to interpret the fire that shall not be quenched in Mark 9: 43-48.

The same principle is seen in Matthew 12:20-21 - A bruised reed shall he not break, and smoking flax shall he not quench till he send forth judgment unto victory. And in his name shall the Gentiles trust.

The Weeping and Gnashing of Teeth

Matthew 8:12 And I say unto you, That many shall come from the east and west, and shall sit down with Abraham, and Isaac, and Jacob, in the kingdom of heaven. But the children of the kingdom shall be cast out into outer darkness: there shall be weeping and gnashing of teeth.

Matthew 22:12-13 And he saith unto him, Friend,

how camest thou in hither not having a wedding garment? And he was speechless. Then said the king to the servants, Bind him hand and foot, and take him away, and cast him into out darkness, there shall be weeping and gnashing of teeth.

Matthew 24:50-51 The lord of that servant shall come in a day when he looketh not for him, and in an hour that he is not aware of, And shall cut him asunder, and appoint him his portion with the hypocrites: there shall be weeping and gnashing of teeth.

Matthew 25: 30-31 And cast ye the unprofitable servant into outer darkness: there shall be weeping and gnashing of teeth. When the Son of man shall come in his glory, and all the holy angels with him, then shall he sit upon the throne of his glory.

Luke 13:27-28 But he shall say, I tell you, I know you not whence ye are; depart from me, all ye workers of iniquity. There shall be weeping and gnashing of teeth, when ye shall see Abraham, and Isaac, and Jacob, and all the prophets, in the kingdom of God, and you yourselves thrust out.

The people experiencing the Outer Darkness, are not unbelievers, but believers who did not seek first the Kingdom of God. This has nothing to do with Going to Hell - or Eternal Damnation. These passages concern our not living in the Light of the Lord, and being in spiritual darkness here on Earth, even if you are a believer.

The children of the kingdom: Those not growing in the Spirit = Going onto Perfection.

A Friend of the King: He was a Friend of the king - not "to" the King. He had no marriage garment. He was still unclean.

The evil servant: He was not looking for the coming of his Lord.

The unprofitable servant: He did not make proper use of the talents his Lord gave him.

Workers of iniquity: They did many works but their Lord did not know them.

Our spiritual journey is from outer darkness to inner light. As we grow in the inner light by the Holy Spirit – we move from the outer darkness of the Soul. Also, the Kingdom of God within the Tabernacle of Moses, is represented by the Holy of Holies.

If we are not Going onto Perfection - we will find ourselves in the Outer Darkness of the Outer Court. To have known that the will of God is to enter the Holy of Holies through fasting, prayer, and meditation of the word of God, and not do it will cause us to be in a state of regret and sorrow - when we see others of the seed of Abraham living in the glory of God.

Abraham, Isaac, and Jacob represent Abraham's seed: If ye be Christ's, then are ye Abraham's seed (Galatians 3:29). This sorrow will be known as - Weeping and Gnashing of Teeth. It may be a figure of speech – or it may be literal.

Hebrews 6: 4-8

This passage terrified me in the past, causing me to fear the possibility of being eternally damned even after becoming a Christian:

> Verses 4-6: For it is impossible for those who were
> once enlightened, and have tasted of the heavenly
> gift, and were made partakers of the Holy Ghost,
> And have tasted the good word of God, and the
> powers of the world (Age) to come, If they shall fall
> away, to renew them again to repentance; <u>seeing</u>
> they crucify to themselves the Son of God afresh,
> and put him to an open shame.

With man not all things are possible – however, with
God, all things are possible (Matthew 19-26). The Greek
word for <u>seeing</u> is – epei, which means – if, or, as long as. It
does not imply a permanent condition. If it did, all things
would not be possible with God. We could forget the
promise of God in Philippians 1:6 "Being confident of this
very thing, that He who began a good work in you will
perform it until the day of Jesus Christ." The Lord restored
Peter after he hardened his heart and denied the Lord three
times. There is no heart so hard that God cannot soften
through the purging fire of His Spirit.

> Verses 7-8: For the earth which drinketh in the rain
> that cometh oft upon it, and bringeth forth herbs
> meet for them by whom it is dressed, receiveth a
> blessing from God: But that which beareth thorns
> and briers is rejected, and is nigh unto cursing;
> whose end is to be burned.

Hard-hearted people are not burned with literal fire –
yet, our God who is a consuming fire, will burn up everything in us, which keeps us from growing deeper into His
presence.

Epiphanies and Apostasies

Jeremiah 2:19 And thy backslidings shall reprove thee.

Hosea 14:4 I will heal their backsliding, I will love them freely: for mine anger is turned away from him..

The Hebrew word for – backsliding, is – Meshubah, which means - Apostasy. God is Love, He will heal the apostasies of the severest Apostates – what an epiphany.

Natural Science
Album: Permanent Waves

I. Tide Pools
When the ebbing tide retreats
Along the rocky shoreline
It leaves a trail of tidal pools
In a short-lived galaxy
Each microcosmic planet
A complete society
A simple kind mirror
To reflect upon our own
All the busy little creatures
Chasing our their destinies
Living in their pools
They soon forget about the sea...

Wheels within wheels
In a spiral array
A pattern so grand
And complex
Time after time
We lose sight of the way
Our causes can't see
Their effects

II. Hyperspace
A quantum leap forward
In time and in space
The universe learned to expand
The mess and the magic
Triumphant and tragic
A mechanized world, out of hand

Computerized clinic
For superior cynics
Who dance to a synthetic band

In their own image
Their world is fashioned -
No wonder they don't understand
Wheels within wheels
In a spiral array
A pattern so grand
And complex
Time after time
We lose sight of the way
Our causes can't see
Their effects

III. Permanent Waves
Science, like nature
Must also be tamed
With a view towards its preservation
Given the same
State of integrity
It will surely serve us well

Art as expression -
Not as market campaigns
Will still capture our imaginations
Given the same
State of integrity
It will surely help us along
The most endangered species -
The honest man
Will still survive annihilation
Forming a world -
State of integrity

Sensitive, open, and strong
Wave after wave
Will flow with the tide
And bury the world as it does
Tide after tide
Will flow and recede
Leaving life to go on
As it was...

CHAPTER THIRTEEN

The Good Judgment of God

Shallow men believe in luck, believe in circumstance -
strong men believe in cause and effect.
- Ralph Waldo Emerson

The Judgment of God is nothing more and nothing less than the Universal Law of Cause and Effect, which is the reason - everything is happening for a reason. It is found in the Bible in Galatians 6:7 Be not deceived; God is not mocked: for whatsoever a man soweth, that shall he also reap.

In 1987, I awoke early one morning to feel the Lord impress on my heart: My judgment flows from my love and mercy to set you free from yourself.

God wants to make us free from all things of darkness and death within us, which inhibit our spiritual growth and ultimately - from obtaining our true inheritance of Immortality. When times are tough and we don't always understand what is going on, encourage yourself with Psalm 145:17 The Lord is righteous in all his ways, and holy in all his works.

The Great White Throne in Revelation 20:11, is a symbol of the omnipresence of God - The Infinite Macrophosphorus. Every hour of every day we stand before the Great White Throne - which is the Judgment Seat of Christ (II Corinthians 5:10), reaping what we have been sowing. The Judgments of God are always corrective in nature. God is Love -He is not a weak, insecure, and vindictive tyrant - waiting for the right moment to slap us down. Yet, there are times when He will slap us down, for our own good:

Isaiah 26:9 When thy judgments are in the earth, the people of the world will learn righteousness.

Matthew 12:20-21 A bruised reed shall he not break, and a smoking flax shall he not quench, till he send forth judgment unto victory. And in his name shall the Gentiles trust.

John 3:19 And this is the judgment, that light is come.

Freewill Balanced by the Golden Rule

How often do we here people say: Hey, who are you to judge? Then sometimes they will quote Matthew 7:1 - Judge not, that ye be not judged. However, Matthew 7:5 says: Thou hypocrite, first cast out the beam out of thine own eye; and then shalt thou see clearly to cast out the mote out of thy brother's eye.

The nature of any judgment that we dispense should be based in the Golden Rule: Therefore all things whatsoever ye would that men should do to you, do ye even so to them: for this is the law and the prophets (Matthew 7:12.).

All the judgment of men in the Earth should be based in this axiom: Freewill Balanced by the Golden Rule. As stated in Chapter One: We should not eat from the Tree of the Knowledge of Good and Evil, but have our senses exercised to discern good and evil, that we might overcome evil with good. The following passages reveal the will of God for us to be good judges in the Earth:

Daniel 7:22 Until the Ancient of days came, and judgment was given to the saints of the Most High; and the time came that the saints possessed the kingdom.

Matthew 19:28 And Jesus said unto them (The Disciples), Verily I say unto you, That ye which have followed me, in the regeneration when the Son of man shall sit in the throne of his glory, ye also shall sit upon the twelve thrones, judging the twelve tribes of Israel.

Luke 22:29-30 And I appoint unto you a kingdom, as my Father hath appointed unto me; That ye may eat and drink at my table in my kingdom, and sit on thrones judging the twelve tribes of Israel.

John 7:24 Judge not according to the appearance, but judge righteous judgment.

I Corinthians 2:15 He that is spiritual judges all things.

I Corinthians 6:2-3 Do ye not know that the saints shall judge the world? and if the world shall be judged by you, are ye unworthy to judge the smallest matters? Know ye not that we shall judge angels? how much more things that pertain to this life?

Revelation 2:27 The overcomers will rule the

nations with a rod of iron.

Revelation 3:21 To him that overcometh will I grant to sit with me in my throne, even as I also overcame, and am set down with my Father in his throne.

The Mount of Olives

Zechariah 14:4 And <u>his feet</u> shall stand in that day upon the mount of Olives, which is before Jerusalem on the east, and the mount of Olives shall cleave in the midst thereof toward the east and toward the west, and there shall be a <u>very great valley</u>, and half of the mountain shall remove toward the north, and half of it toward the south.

The Bible often uses different scenarios to depict a single event. The dividing of the Mount of Olives, is also spiritually discerned in the following three portions of the Word of God:

1. Multitudes in the Valley of Decision (Joel 3:14).

2. The Sons of Zadok (Order of Melchizedek) shall come in controversy, dividing the Holy and the Profane, the Clean and the Unclean (Ezekiel 44: 23-24).

3. The Dividing of the Sheep and Goats (Matthew 25: 31-46).

It is clear from II Thessalonians 1:7-10, that the coming of Jesus is within the saints. He shall judge the world through the remnant of the Body of Christ that takes the lead in this reality, they are called - His Feet:

Psalm 47:3 He shall subdue the people under us, and the nations under our feet.

Ephesians 1:22-23 And He hath put all things under his feet, and gave him to be the head over all things TO THE CHURCH, Which is his body, the fullness of him that filleth all in all.

The Divine Dividing

Zechariah 14:12 says - Their flesh (earthly nature) shall consume away while they stand on their feet, and their eyes (unspiritual vision) shall consume away in their holes, and their tongues (vain speech) shall consume away in their mouth.

This will happen as the polarities of the Word of God are revealed. Jesus Christ – through the Order of Melchizedek = His Royal Priesthood, shall divide the Sheep and Goats. This dividing shall also reveal the following scriptural dualities in the Bible, which are synonymous by association:

The Goats VS The Sheep
Babylon VS Zion
The Whore VS The Bride
Apathy VS Love
Carnal Mind VS Spiritual Mind
Some Things Happen For a Reason VS Everything is Happening For A Reason
Jesus Christ has some authority VS Jesus Christ has All authority
We Meditate VS We are being Meditated
Death VS Life

Darkness VS Light
Religion VS Spirituality
Cursed VS Blessed
Sowing to the Flesh VS Sowing to the Spirit
Levitical Priesthood VS The Order of Melchizedek
The Kings of the Earth VS The Kings of the East
Unspiritual interpretations of Bible VS Spiritual interpretations
of Bible
Restoration of Some Things VS The Restoration of All Things
Wolves in Sheep's Clothing VS The True Shepherds
Lies, Omissions, Illusion, Deception VS The Truth
Eternal Damnation doctrines VS The Abrahamic Covenant
Tree of the Knowledge of Good and Evil VS The Tree of Life
Profane VS Holy
Anti-Christ VS Christ
Pleasing men VS Pleasing the Lord
The Rapture VS Salvation – Spirit, Soul, and Body
Mortality VS Immortality
Fear VS Faith
Old Earth VS New Earth
The First Man=The Old Man VS The Second Man=The New Man
Not going unto perfection VS Going unto perfection
Lukewarm VS Hot for Jesus
Traditions of men VS The Foundation of Apostles and Prophets
Unclean VS Clean
Image of the Beast VS The Image of Christ
Tickling Ears VS Ears to Hear
Five Foolish Virgins VS Five Wise Virgins
Indecision VS Decision

If you choose not to decide, you still have made a choice.
- Neil Peart

The preceding quote is from the song - Freewill, on the
Rush album - Permanent Waves, which I believe is nicely

applicable. I am not suggesting that Neil Peart wrote this lyric with the preceding polarities in mind.

Tai Shan
Album: Hold Your Fire

High on the sacred mountain
Up the seven thousand stairs
In the golden light of autumn
There was magic in the air

Clouds surrounded the summit
The wind blew strong and cold
Among the silent temples
And the writings carved in gold
Somewhere in my instincts
The primitive took hold...

I stood at the top of the mountain
And China sang to me
In the peaceful haze of harvest time
A song of eternity –

If you raise your hands to heaven
You will live a hundred years
I stood there like a mystic
Lost in the atmosphere

The clouds were suddenly parted
For a moment I could see
The patterns of the landscape
Reaching to the eastern sea
I looked upon a presence
Spanning forty centuries

I thought of time and distance
The hardships of history
I heard the hope and the hunger
When China sang to me...

CHAPTER FOURTEEN

The New Earth

There is an invisible world out there and we are living in it.
- Bill Viola

I recall watching David Frost interviewing Ted Turner, the Founder of CNN. At one point in the interview, as they were discussing the topic of religion, Ted said – "Sitting around on a cloud playing a harp for all eternity doesn't hold a lot of attraction for me, but if I could fly–fish, and live in a little cabin in the mountains, I could go for that."

As we rendezvous with Mother Nature, whether skiing the Colorado back–country under a deep blue sky, lounging along an ocean shore, walking through autumn woods, or gazing into the midnight sky of a desert expanse, it's natural to feel we are experiencing heaven on earth. We have been closer to the truth than we have imagined. This planet we inhabit is our – Home, Sweet Home.

The New Earth is when Heaven and Earth become One.

Heaven + Earth = The New Earth.

The New Earth is not a new planet that will suddenly

appear out of the deep-space of a parallel universe, as our current planet is consumed by nuclear fire, or any other cunningly devised fables that have been passed on to us. Alternately, God is now in the process of restoring the earth with His Presence. Psalm 72:19 sounds the knell against the darkness: "Let the whole earth be filled with his glory; Amen and Amen." The prophet Habakkuk broadcasted: "For the whole earth shall be filled with the knowledge of the glory of the Lord, as the waters cover the sea" (Habakkuk 2:14). We are now living in the days of the - times of refreshing from the presence of the Lord and the Restoration of All Things (Acts 3:19-26). The Spirit of the Lord is bringing us back to the days of heaven on earth (Deuteronomy 11:21).

The end of the world – is not the end of our planet as we have been taught by some. The end of the world, is the end of our mortal perception of the world – it begins with believing ETHFAR. Jesus Christ lived in the New Earth during His earthly sojourn, we know He believed every-thing was happening for a reason, in that - He did not enter into sin by eating from the Tree of the Knowledge of Good and Evil (Genesis 2:17 and Hebrews 4:15). Rather, He ate from the Tree of Life - overcoming evil with good. We also begin to live in the New Earth, as our earthly nature conforms to the Word of God by the renewing of our imaginations.

What's New?

A New Cart for the Ark of the Covenant (II Samuel 6:3).
A New Garment (I Kings 11:29-30).
A New Thing in the Earth…A women shall compass a man (Jeremiah 31:22).
A New Spirit (Ezekiel 11:19).

New Bottles (Mark 2:22).
New Tongues (Mark 6:17).
New Wine (Joel 3:18).
A New Creation (II Corinthians 5:17).
The New Man (Ephesians 4:24).
A New Country (Hebrews 11:16).
A New Name (Revelation 2:17).
The New Jerusalem (Revelation 3:12).
A New Song (Revelation 5:9).
The New Heavens and New Earth (Revelation 21:1).
All Things Made New (Revelation 21:5).

New things do I declare (Isaiah 42:9).

Behold, I shall do a new thing, now it shall spring forth (Isaiah 43:19).

I showed thee new things, even hidden things, and you did not know them (Isaiah 48:6).

I will do a work in your days, which you will not believe (Habakkuk 1:5).

The New Earth

Isaiah 51:16 I have put my words in thy mouth and covered thee in the shadow of mine hand, that I may plant the heavens, and lay the foundations of the earth, and say unto Zion, thou art my people.

Isaiah 65:17 For behold, I create new heavens and a new earth: and the former things shall not be remembered, nor come to mind.

Isaiah 66:22 The new heavens and the new earth shall remain before me.

When the Bible speaks of the New Heavens, it is alluding to new spiritual dimensions we shall stride in as we grow more deeply into the presence of the Lord. The New Earth is two-fold: Our earthen temple will be renewed as we walk further into the presence of Jesus. Secondly, our planet Earth will again be covered in the translucent brilliance of the Glory of Our Creator.

II Peter 3:13 According to his promise, we look for the new heavens and the new earth wherein dwells righteousness.

This oracle says: We look for the new heavens and the new earth - it does not say: We will look or we shall look. God is not telling us to begin gazing through a telescope, searching the midnight sky for a new heaven and a new planet called Earth. Rather, He wants us seeking His presence so that He may radically alter our internal and external experience. Jesus said: "My words are spirit and life." God loves us all and wants to pour out the richness of His presence on us now. Do not let fairy-tale theology devalue your life here on Earth. Don't listen to those false prophets out there - that "make you vain" (Jeremiah 23:16).

And I saw a new heaven and a new earth: for the first heaven and the first earth were passed away, and there was no more sea.
- Revelation 21:1

To understand the practical application of this passage, it is imperative that we remain in the Biblical framework for our spiritual growth - The Tabernacle of Moses. The new heaven and new earth is the realm of the Holy of Holies - The Third Heaven. The first heaven and earth that pass away is our limited spiritual experience in the Holy Place - the Second Heaven.

More to the point, within the context of the Book of Revelation, the Holy Place (not the Outer Court), is considered the first heaven that passes away. Revelation 11:2 states: "But the court (The Outer Court) which is without the temple leave out, and measure it not, for it is given unto the Gentiles." Jesus deals with the Overcomers - His Bride, in the Holy Place, until she arrives in the Holy of Holies.

This same principle is found in Hebrews 9:2-3: For there was a tabernacle made, the first, wherein was the candlestick, and the table, and the shewbread; which is called the sanctuary. And after the second veil, the tabernacle which is called the Holiest of all.

Hebrews 9:6-8 reinforces this same thought: Now when these things were thus ordained, the priests went always into the first tabernacle, accomplishing the service of God. But into the second went the high priest alone once every year, not without blood, which he offered for himself, and for the errors of the people. The Holy Ghost this signifying, that the way into the holiest of all was not yet made manifest, while as the first tabernacle was yet standing.

Alarmingly, John 2:23-25 records: Now when he was in Jerusalem at the Passover (Which is synonymous with the Outer Court experience) in the feast day, many believed in his name, when they saw the miracles which he did. But Jesus did not commit himself unto them, because he knew all men, And needed not that any should testify of man: for he knew what was in man.

The Book of Revelation - is the Revelation of Jesus Christ (Revelation 1:1). He is being revealed in those that pursue Him with all of their heart and mind. Those that merely play church, and are satisfied that they are Born-Again, refusing to

Go Onto Perfection, shall remain in the Outer Court.

"No more sea" in Revelation 21:1 means, there shall be no more turbulence of the Old Man = The Old Earth, within us - because, the peace of the presence of God = The New Man = The New Earth, floods our being. Living in the New Earth, is also when the dreams and visions that God has given you, become one with your reality = Xanadu.

Heaven in the Bible

Without reservation I make this statement: Heaven is the Presence of God.

Our Creator created Earth to be our Paradise. I once felt the Lord impress on me - Is the paradise of my presence not good enough for you?

There is no Hawaii in the Sky, or geographical location with pearly gates, golden streets, white celestial sands, and translucent palm trees, that we are to fantasize and daydream about called HEAVEN. If there is, there is no reference to it in the Bible. Revelation 21:21, speaking of the New Jerusalem, states: "*And the street of the city was pure gold, as it were transparent glass.*" The street of gold is a metaphorical representation of walking in the glory of the Lord, moving beyond our humanity and into our divinity. Or, putting off the Old Man = Adam, and putting on the New Man = Christ.

Ephesians 2:6-7 is a profound revelation, it says, God - Hath raised us up together, and made us sit together in heavenly places in Christ Jesus, that in the ages to come he might shew the exceeding riches of his grace in his kindness toward us through Jesus Christ.

This passage says – "we are seated in heavenly places." It does not say – "up in heaven someday the Lord will bless us." It says, In the ages to come = through the endlessness of

Time and Space – here on Earth.

Heaven is here now because the presence of God is here now. Heaven is the Glory of God. If Heaven is a three-dimensional location to be obtained after we die, what need is there to Go onto Perfection? It's time to do away with Alice in Wonderland theology - which only drives us into the yawning beds of spiritual slumber. There is no better way to do it, than to open the Bible:

John 3:13 No man has ascended up to heaven, but he that came down from heaven, even the Son of man which is in heaven.

The reason Jesus could walk on the water, heal the sick, raise the dead, and perform so many miracles is that he was living in Heaven on Earth. Jesus did so many miracles that John wrote:

And there are also many other things which Jesus did, the which, if they were written every one, I suppose that even the world itself could not contain the books that should be written. Amen (John 21:25).

John 12:26 Where I am, there shall my servants be.

If we were walking the sandy shores of the Sea of Galilee with Jesus, and asked Him: What do you mean - where you are? He would have said: Oh, I'm living in the heavenlies.

John 14:2-3 In my Father's house are many mansions: if it were not so, I would have told you. I go to prepare a place for you. And if I go to prepare a place for you, I will come again, and receive you unto myself; that where I am, there ye may be also.

Notice Jesus said: "Where I am." He did not say – "Where I was" or "Where I will be." God wants us living in the same dimension of the Spirit realm that Jesus was in, when He walked on the Earth – so that, we can be free from darkness and death, and then deliver humanity.

The Lord does have a mansion for you - a specific realm in His presence that He has designed just for you. At the same time, this spiritual reality will manifest in the natural – to keep the New Earth, down to earth - consider Isaiah 65:21 "And they shall build houses, and inhabit them; and they shall plant vineyards, and eat the fruit of them." That sure makes the mystical - practical. Life goes on in the New Earth.

John 17:11 And now, I am no more in the world, but these are in the world.

What did Jesus mean by - "I am no longer in this world?" Did He mean - He was no longer into fleshly things? — He never was! In John 17:1 Jesus prayed to the Father – "Glorify thy Son." When Jesus prayed, He believed that he had received (Mark 11:24). He was caught up into a higher realm of the presence of God – a higher realm of Heaven.

John 17:24 Father, I will that they also, whom thou hast given me, <u>be with me where I am.</u>

Ephesians 2:6 God has raised us up with him, and seated us with him in heavenly places, in Christ Jesus.

Heavenly places are in Heaven. There are many spiritual dimensions in the presence of God.

Philippians 3:20 For our citizenship is in heaven

from whence also we look for our Saviour, the Lord Jesus Christ.

From the study of The Tabernacle of Moses, we know the Outer Court is the First Heaven and the Holy Place is the Second Heaven. Hence, it is from these two Heavenly places that we look for Christ in the Holy of Holies - the Third Heaven, that we might be fully conformed to His image, that he might fully deliver us from mortality - Spirit, Soul, and Body.

Where do people go when they die?

Ecclesiastes 12:7 Then shall the dust return to the earth as it was: and the spirit shall return unto God who gave it.

I am not untouched by the passing on of loved ones. In this last thirteen months I have suffered the loss of my Mother, Step-Father, Grandmother, Aunt, and this morning - February 18, 2004, I just heard my cousin passed away. I just finished making the phone calls to Family members, and am still in shock, with tears in my eyes. Yet, I believe they have all passed on to their next stage of spiritual evolution in the presence of God. This is how I frame it. To say - *they died*, seems negative and defeated to me when I know their spirit (who they really are) is with Jesus.

At the memoriam for my Mother, I shared Hebrew 12:1 with family and friends: *Wherefore seeing we also are compassed about with so great a cloud of witnesses, let us lay aside every weight, and the sin which doth so easily beset us, and let us run with patience the race that is set before us.* Then I added – "If that is true, my Mom is listening to everything going on here today - so in unison, let's say - we love you Jan" – and they did. Amen.

Heaven is the Paradise which is spoken of in the Bible – which is the presence of God, who is omnipresent in both the visible and invisible realms. I Kings 8:27 says: "Behold, the heaven and heaven of heavens cannot contain thee." If the physical body dies, the spirit has no choice but to return to God. It is the physical body and darkness in the mind that separates us from the fact that God is omni-existent.

If we do not obtain immortality on Earth, then shall the dust return to the earth as it was: and the spirit shall return unto God who gave it. The spirit of a person will return back into the infinite light, life, and love that God is. Romans 11:36 states: "For out of him, and through him, and to him are all things." Jesus told the thief on the cross next to him: "Verily I say unto thee, 'Today shalt thou be with me in paradise" (Luke 23:43) - the paradise of the presence of God.

To get down to the nuts-and-bolts of it – where are the passages in the Bible which refer to this place called Heaven? Some suppose Heaven is found in Revelation 21:21 - *"And the twelve gates were twelve pearls; every gate was of one pearl: and the street of the city was pure gold, as it was transparent glass."* However, this verse speaks of the New Jerusalem, who is the Bride of Christ, descending <u>out of heaven</u> from God (Revelation 21:9-10).

The next passage we might imagine, is found in the parable of Lazarus and the Rich Man - *"And it came to pass, that the beggar died, and was carried by the angels into Abraham's bosom: the rich man also died, and was buried"*(Luke 16:22). It has been assumed that Abraham's Bosom is Heaven. However, if this is true, what happened to Abel, Seth, Enoch, and Noah - men of God that died before Abraham? This parable is a narration of the election of grace in the New Covenant (Lazarus), and the doing away with Old Covenant (The Rich Man). This is touched upon in the chapter twelve - Hell: The Cruel Illusion.

Is Reincarnation in the Bible?

Reincarnation is an issue that many churches have not honestly addressed. They diss it as *New Age Eastern Philosophy*, while disregarding the fact that the Bible is a book that originated in the East. Once again – what saith the Word of the Lord:

> Matthew 11:12-14 And from the days of John the Baptist until now the kingdom of heaven suffereth violence, and the violent take it by force. For all the prophets and the law prophesied until John. And if ye will receive it, this is Elias (Elijah), which was for to come. He that hath ears to hear, let him hear.

John the Baptist denied twice that he was Elijah (John 1:21). Yet, Jesus said he was Elijah – who should we believe? John the Baptist or The Lord Jesus Christ?

Jesus said, "If ye will receive it." Most in the church will not receive the truth of Elijah being reincarnated as John the Baptist – it becomes a road-block to their bogus doctrines of eternal damnation. Of reincarnation, Jesus said – He that hath ears let him hear.

In the effort to avoid reincarnation, many preachers cut and run to Hebrew 9:27 "As it is appointed unto men once to die, but after this the judgment." It was Adam that appointed men once to die, then the judgment. They freely assume the judgment is standing before God at the Great White Throne some day up in Heaven. However, the judgment is qualified in the next verse - Hebrews 9:28: "So Christ was once offered to bear the sins of many; and unto them that look for him shall he appear the second time without sin unto salvation."

Resurrection or Reincarnation

The reason reincarnation is not a large issue in the Bible is this - God wants us to step off the merry-go-round of Life and Death, and Go Onto Perfection pursuing the Resurrection in us – Spirit, Soul, and Body. We see the reality of this on the Mount of Transfiguration in the seventeenth chapter of Matthew - when Moses and Elias appeared with Jesus, talking with him (Verses 1-3).

Moses represented the Law, and to the disciples, Elijah represented reincarnation - because of the news of John the Baptist. To ensure the disciples had their focus in the right place, the heavenly Father spoke to them in Matthew 17:5 – While he yet spake, behold, a bright cloud overshadowed them: and behold a voice out of the cloud, which said, This is my beloved Son, in whom I am well pleased; hear ye him.

God the Father did not want the disciples focusing on the Law or Reincarnation – He wanted their focus to be on Jesus, the Resurrection. On the way down the mountain, Jesus told Peter, James, and John in Matthew 17: 12-13 - But I say unto you, That Elias is come already, and they knew him not, but have done unto him whatsoever they listed. Likewise shall also the Son of man suffer of them. Then the disciples understood that he spake unto them of John the Baptist.

In Conclusion: If we do not put on immortality, we will physically die. Then our spirit will return to God. Because God wants three-dimensional expressions of His Spirit in the Earth (read Chapter Two), it is foolish to assume that after a spirit has returned to the Lord, that He would not consider placing that spirit in a womb at another time.

There is no scripture that precludes the possibility of reincarnation. However, it is not the highest will of God. Jesus was speaking of himself in John 6:58: This is that bread which came down from heaven: not as your fathers did eat manna <u>and are dead</u>: he that eateth of this bread shall live for ever.

As the presence of God increases around the Earth, people will begin to live longer. Isaiah 65:20 reads: There shall be no more thence an infant of days, nor an old man that hath not filled his days: for the child shall die an hundred years old; but the sinner being an hundred years old shall be accursed.

The Analog Kid
Album: Signals

A hot and windy August afternoon
Has the trees in constant motion
With a flash of silver leaves
As they're rocking in the breeze

The boy lies in the grass with one blade
Stuck between his teeth
A vague sensation quickens
In his young and restless heart
And a bright and nameless vision
Has him longing to depart

You move me –
You move me –
With your buildings and your eyes
Autumn woods and winter skies
You move me –
You move me –
Open sea and city lights
Busy streets and dizzy heights
You call me –
You call me –

The fawn-eyed girl with sun-browned legs
Dances on the edge of his dream
And her voice rings in his ears
Like the music of the spheres

The boy lies in the grass, unmoving
Staring at the sky
His mother starts to call him
As a hawk goes soaring by
The boy pulls down his baseball cap
And covers up his eyes

Too many hands on my time
To many feelings –
Too many things on my mind
When I leave I don't know
What I'm hoping to find
When I leave I don't know
What I'm leaving behind…

CHAPTER FIFTEEN

The Queen of the South

You can't force the blossoming of a rose.
- Frances Roberts

Matthew 12:42 and Luke 11:31 archive the mysterious account of Jesus prophesying of the Queen of the South. He declared the decree that she would rise up in judgment with the men of this generation, and condemn them. Within these two synonymous verses, the Queen of Sheba is used as a type of the Queen of the South who came to hear the wisdom of Solomon. Then Jesus said, "A greater than Solomon is here." The Queen of the South in this era, and throughout eternity, is the Bride of Christ.

Mary, the sister of Martha, was a figure of the Queen of the South. As the Queen of Sheba came to hear the wisdom of Solomon, so also, when Martha was overly concerned with household distractions, Mary sat at the feet of Jesus to hear his word. Jesus said: "One thing is needful, and Mary hath chosen that good part, which will not be taken from her" (Luke 10-38-42). It has been said: *God has a lot of*

275

children, but not a lot of friends. Those that continually yearn for an intimate love affair with Jesus are His Bride – His Dream Lover - Mrs. Jesus Christ - Mrs. The Word of God (Revelation 19:13).

> Jesus is the Bridegroom – His true disciples are His Bride.
> Jesus is the King of Kings – His Bride is the Queen of Queens.
> Jesus is the Emperor - His Bride is the Empress.
> Jesus is the King of Peace - His Bride is the Queen of Peace.
> Jesus is God – His Bride is a Goddess.
> Jesus is the Duke – His Bride is his Duchess in His Dukedom.
> Jesus is the High Priest after the Order of Melchizedek - His Bride is the High Priestess after the Order of Melchizedek.

Positionally, in the Spirit, the Body of Christ is the Bride of Christ. However, it takes time for the existential and experiential to become one. When the spiritual reality of who we are in Jesus actualizes in the natural, then we will see the prophecies spoken of in the Book of Revelation concerning the Overcomers exhibited in the Earth.

In Revelation 18:4 Jesus says: "Come out of her, my people." The Bride has no association with the Whore – that she may remain unencumbered in her love affair with Jesus; that she may Go onto Perfection in His presence (Hebrews 6:1).

> Revelation 18:23: (Of Babylon – The Great Whore) And the light of a candle shall shine no more at all in thee; and the voice of the bridegroom and of the bride shall be heard no more at all in thee: for thy

merchants were the great men of the earth, for by thy sorceries were all nations deceived.

The Bride Makes Herself Ready

Let us be glad and rejoice, and give honour to him: for the marriage of the Lamb is come, and <u>his wife hath made herself ready</u>. And to her was granted that she should be arrayed in fine linen, clean and white: for the fine linen is the righteousness of the saints. And he saith unto me, Write, Blessed are they which are called unto the marriage supper of the Lamb. And he saith unto me, These are the true sayings of God (Revelation 19:7-9).

I Corinthians 6:17 says: "He that is joined to the Lord is one spirit." When we are Born Again, our spirit becomes one with the Holy Spirit. As we move forward into conformity with the heavenly image (I Corinthians 15:49), which is being conformed into the image of Christ (Romans 8:29) this is when our Spirit and Soul begin to become one. The Lord gives us a metaphorical oracle of this reality in the nineteenth chapter of the book of Revelation.

Contrary to widespread opinion, the marriage supper of the Lamb is not a future event up in a Heaven someplace beyond the far reaches of outer-space. The Bible is a spiritual book, inspired by the Holy Spirit, for our spiritual growth – this holds true for the Book of Revelation. The Bible says: "The marriage of the Lamb is come." The marriage of the Lamb is the union of our Spirit (The Bridegroom) and our Soul (The Bride).

This is anti-climatic for those that live in the flesh, who prefer to center their attentions on the alleged drama about to take place in natural Israel in the Last Days. However, for those who have made Jesus their first love, and want to move deeper into the sacred realms of the sweet repose of

His presence, this is the true interpretation.

> Colossians 3:1-2 If ye be risen with Christ, seek those things which are above, where Christ sitteth on the right hand of God. Set your affection on things above, not on things on the earth.

The way the Bride - the Lamb's Wife, makes herself ready, for the marriage of the Lamb which is come - is to wine and dine at the marriage supper by implementing the three key elements of her spiritual growth, which are:

Fasting
Praying in the Spirit
Meditating the Word of God

Fasting

The sacred secret of the sanctuary to actualize the ever-increasing ascension of the glory of Jesus Christ within us – to live in the opening of the heavens of His presence, is fasting. Those that partake of the Feast of Fasting will find themselves experiencing an increase of faith, power, and the gifts of the Holy Spirit (I Corinthians 12: 4-11). Those that speak against fasting, are merely a mouthpiece of the vacuous nature of the decadent mind, "whose God is their belly, and whose glory is in their shame, who mind earthly things" (Philippians 3:19). The following passages support this essential element in the preparation of the Bride:

> Mark 2:20 But the days will come, when the bridegroom is taken from them, and then shall they fast in those days.

They who fast for the increase of the presence of Jesus, the Bridegroom, are the Bride.

Luke 4:14 And Jesus returned in the power of the Spirit into Galilee: and there went out a fame of him through all the region round about.

Jesus returned in the power of the glory of God after he had fasted for forty days.

Isaiah 58:8 Then shall thy light break forth as the morning, and thy health shall spring forth speedily: and thy righteousness shall go before thee; and the glory of the Lord shall be thy reward.

The whole chapter of Isaiah 58 is concerning fasting. This is the preparation of the Bride chapter, directly preceding the glory that we shall experience in the last seven chapters of Isaiah.

Psalm 35:13b I humbled my soul with fasting: and my prayer returned to my bosom.

Many times we don't feel like praying, when we do, we feel like our prayers go no higher than the ceiling – this is because the flesh is too strong. Fasting clears out the darkness of the mind as the Spirit of God begins to ascend, which is the presence of God dawning within our hearts. This is what David meant by: "My prayer returned to my bosom." He was praying out of his spirit – not out of his soulish nature. When we fast, we move out of our natural consciousness into the supernatural consciousness of the Lord. Fasting is a way of putting off the old man, and putting on the new man.

In Daniel Chapter One - Daniel, Hananiah, Mishael, and

Azariah, fasted for ten days. After the fast, the Bible says: Their countenances appeared fairer and fatter in flesh than all the children which did eat meat. God gave them knowledge, skill in learning, and wisdom; Daniel had understanding in all visions and dreams. Nebuchadnezzar the King of Babylon, found them ten times better than all the magicians and astrologers that were in his realm (Daniel 1:11-20).

Because fasting is free, and unpopular, you won't find many people talking about it. The Bible says: "When we fast we are to read the words of the Lord" (Jeremiah 36:6). This will keep our minds focused – listen to your heart and ask God to give you wisdom on how to fast. If you have never fasted before, you may have some physical discomfort and headaches within the first 48 hours. Be encouraged, this is your body telling you that toxins are being released out of your system. Drinking water with lemon in it, will assist your body in cleaning itself. When you break the fast, eat a piece of fruit, let your digestive system slowly back into the digestive process. Do not gorge yourself with a huge Mexican dinner.

A book that has been an emerald gem to me over the years for inspiration and learning how to fast, was written by Paul Bragg, the title of the book is: *The Miracle of Fasting*. It can be ordered through major bookstores such as Barnes & Noble and Borders, you can also contact Bragg Life Foods directly in Santa Barbara, California at 1-800-446-1990, or, order the book on their website at www.bragg.com.

Praying in the Spirit

Praying in the Spirit or Praying in Tongues – is the gift of God for us to strengthen our spirit so that we can have increased faith and power, that we might live in the immortal presence of God, being glorified with Him (Romans

8:17-18). It is not only a sign of the Baptism in the Holy Spirit, it is the purpose of the Baptism in the Holy Spirit. The following scriptures reveal the will of God for Praying in the Spirit:

Isaiah 28:11 For with stammering lips and another tongue will he speak to this people.

Mark 16:17 And these signs shall follow them that believe; In my name shall they cast out devils; they shall speak with new tongues.

Romans 8:26 Likewise the Spirit also helpeth our infirmities: for we know not what we should pray for as we ought: but the Spirit itself maketh intercession for us with groanings which cannot be uttered.

Hebrews 7:25 Wherefore he is able also to save them to the uttermost (Salvation: Spirit, Soul, and Body) that come unto God by him, seeing he ever liveth to make intercession for them.

Jesus lives to intercede within us by the Holy Spirit, through Praying in the Spirit.

I Corinthians 2:6-7 Howbeit we speak wisdom among them that are perfect: yet not the wisdom of the world, nor of the princes of this world, that come to nought (that die): But we speak the wisdom of God in a mystery, even the hidden wisdom, which God ordained before the world unto our glory.

Jude 20-21 But ye beloved, building yourselves up on your most holy faith, praying in the Holy Ghost, Keeping yourself in the love of God, looking for the mercy of our Lord Jesus Christ unto eternal life (The life of the ages).

Ephesians 6:17-18a And take the helmet of salvation, and the sword of the Spirit, which is the word of God: Praying always with all prayer and supplication in the Spirit.

There are wolves in sheep's clothing today that say: "Speaking in tongues no longer exists," then quote I Corinthians 13: 8 "tongues shall cease." - They have not ceased yet, I still pray in tongues and I know others that do as well. When will tongues cease? Maybe after we have put on immortality (I Corinthians 15:53). Other wolves quote I Corinthians 12:30 "do all speak with tongues?" They use this scripture as a way out – they are in fear that their congregation might get out of hand. Therefore, no one speaks in tongues – they remain the frozen chosen.

The Apostle Paul spoke by God the Father when he said: "Forbid not to speak in tongues." (I Corinthians 14:39). He said, " I thank my God I speak with tongues more than you all" (I Corinthians 14:18). I Corinthians chapters 12 and 14 are the two big chapters on speaking in tongues and the other gifts of the Holy Spirit. There needs to be discernment when Paul is talking about Tongues in the church setting, and being alone with the Lord.

Baptizing Yourself in the Holy Spirit

It is the will of God for everyone on the planet to be Baptized in the Holy Spirit and Pray in the Spirit - so that our spirit can ascend in the power of God. In Acts 2:4 it says: They were all filled with the Holy Ghost, and began to speak with other tongues, as the Spirit gave them utterance.

If you were there, you would have been filled with the Holy Spirit also, and begun speaking in tongues. Jesus is not holding anything of His Spirit back from you. Ephesians 1:3 declares: Blessed be the God and Father of our Lord Jesus Christ, who hath blessed us with all spiritual blessings in heavenly places in Christ.

The way the Lord has shown me to pray for people to receive the Baptism in the Holy Spirit and the gift of Tongues is this: Lead them through a prayer to receive the Baptism, place your hand on their stomach, believing for the river of living waters to begin springing up out of their spirit.

To elevate their mind out of the natural and into the supernatural, have them repeat some of the words that the Holy Spirit prays through you. For instance - Ask them to pray, "Lord Jesus, I worship you as my Lord and Saviour, I ask you now to Baptize me in your Holy Spirit. (Have them lift their hands to heaven and believe Jesus NOW to flow forth through them in the intercession of the Spirit). Begin praying in the Spirit and tell them to repeat some of the words the Lord is speaking through you, for example:

Ko Dah Buh Sun Dah —Ver Rah Shun Dah Buh Sun Dah...

Keep repeating these syllables, until you feel other words flowing out of you.

The gift of Praying in Tongues is the will of God for everyone on the planet. If you approach the Lord with a sincere heart, in faith, knowing it is His will, the Lord shall bless you in this way. The Lord may give you just a few syllables at first. Let them flow – the more you let the Holy Spirit pray through you, the stronger you will become in the Spirit. You will have more joy and wisdom; more faith and clarity - on the things that concern you. You will be on your way to living deeper in the Glory of the Lord.

Praying in the Spirit will build up your faith, so that when you pray in the natural, your prayers will be filled with words of faith and prophetic power. You will have the "testimony of Jesus which is the spirit of prophecy" (Revelation 19:10). You will prophesy unto the mountains in your life - Be Removed! And they will be cast into the sea, because you are believing that you have received (Mark 11:23-24). You will overflow in expectation by the power of the Holy Spirit (Romans 15:13). This is living in the "Voice of the Day of the Lord" (Zephaniah 1:14).

Amos 3:8 The lion hath roared, who will not fear? the Lord God hath spoken, who can but prophesy?

Meditating The Word

As we fast and pray in the Holy Ghost – with the testimony of Jesus, it is important to keep the images in our mind in the will of God, by meditating in His incorruptible Word. This is being conformed unto the image of Christ (Romans 8:29).

Jeremiah 1:12 God watches over His word to perform it.

Proverbs 4:20-22 My Son, attend to my words; incline thine ears unto my sayings. Let them not depart from the eyes; keep them in the midst of thine heart. For they are life unto those that find them, and health to all their flesh.

Psalm 1:2-3 But his delight is in the law of the Lord; and in his law doth he meditate day and night. And he shall be like a tree planted by the rivers of water, that bringeth forth his fruit in his season; his leaf also shall not wither; and whatsoever he doeth shall prosper.

James 1:25 But whoso looketh into the perfect law of liberty, and continues therein, he being not a forgetful hearer, but a doer of the work, this man will be blessed in his deed.

Note: The doing of the work is meditating in the word – then you will be blessed in your deeds.

Psalm 119 – All of it.

II Peter 1:19 We have a more sure word of prophecy; whereunto ye do well that ye take heed, as unto a light that shineth in a dark place, until the day dawn, and the day star arise in your heart.

Colossians 3:16 Let the word of Christ dwell in you richly in all wisdom; teaching and admonishing one another in psalms and hymns and spiritual songs, singing with grace in your hearts to the Lord.

The Joy of the Lord

As we are praying in the Spirit, the joy of the Lord begins swelling in our being. Let it flow out as the Bible says - in praise, worship, and spiritual songs. Psalm 22:3 heralds: But thou art holy, O thou that inhabits the praises of Israel.

Psalm 16:11 In God's presence is the fullness of joy.

Numbers 32:32 They crossed over Jordan armed in the presence of the Lord.

Isaiah 63:9 The angel of His presence saved them.

Psalm 43:4 God is my exceeding joy.

Psalm 51:12 Restore unto me the joy of thy salvation; and uphold me with thy free spirit.

Nehemiah 8:10 The joy of the Lord is your strength.

Jeremiah 33:11 The voice of joy and gladness is the voice of the Bridegroom and Bride.

John 15:11 These things have I spoken to you that my joy might remain in you, and that your joy may be full.

Romans 14:17 The kingdom of God is not meat and drink, but righteousness, peace, and joy in the Holy Ghost.

Jude 24 He shall present you faultless before the presence of his glory with exceeding joy.

The New Jerusalem

It is clear from Revelation 21:9-11, that the New Jerusalem is the Bride of Jesus Christ:

And there came unto me on the seven angels which had the seven vials full of the seven last plagues, and talked with me, saying, Come hither, I will shew thee the bride, the Lamb's wife. And he carried me away in the spirit to a great and high mountain (Mount Zion), and shewed me that great city, the holy Jerusalem, descending out of heaven from God, Having the glory of God: and her light was like unto a stone most precious, even like a jasper stone, clear as crystal.

The ascension of Jesus within the castle of our consciousness is equated as the descension of the New Jerusalem out of Heaven from God. In other words, our spiritual ascension into the presence of God - which is Heaven, is also the descension of the Holy Spirit into the lower realm of our Soul.

As this is occurring, (from glory to glory - II Corinthians 3:18), we are transformed from Christ being merely in us - the hope of glory (Colossians 1:27) into the Bride – having the glory (Revelation 21:11). When the Bride has fully arrived into the fullness of the presence of the Bridegroom, she is then crowned - The Queen of the South.

The Overcomers are the Bride which is the New Jerusalem. Revelation 3:11-13 declares:

Behold, I come quickly: hold fast which thou hast, that no man take thy crown. Him that overcometh will I make a pillar in the temple of my God; and he shall go no more out: and I will write upon him the name of my God, which is the name of the city of my God, which is the new Jerusalem, which cometh down out of heaven from my God: and I will write upon him my new name. He that hath an ear, let him hear what the Spirit saith unto the churches.

Holy, holy, holy, Lord God Almighty, which was, and is, and is to come.

- Revelation 4:8b

Printed in the United States
17873LVS00001B/7